h open eyes." —T.E. Lawrence "The master in the art of living makes little distinction between his work and his play, his
mply pursues his vision of excellence at whatever he does, leaving others to decide whether he is working or playing. To hir
e "In the land of the blind, the one-eyed man is king." —Desiderius Erasmus "D   you have where
o keep, and miles to go before I sleep, and miles to go before I sleep." —Ro   appens to you a
ers of the night, who in the dusty recesses of their mind, dream and wake in t   vanity. But the
living makes little distinction between his work and his play, his labor and his   y, his informat
eaving others to decide whether he is working or playing. To him, he's always d   g both." —James A. Michener "We are
siderius Erasmus "Do what you can with what you have where you are." —Theodore Roosevelt "That's a BB in a boxcar."
I sleep." —Robert Frost "Life is 10% what happens to you and 90% how you respond to it." —Bill's Grandmother Harris
nd wake in the morning to find it was just vanity. But the Dreamers of the Day are dangerous people because they act their
his labor and his leisure, his mind and his body, his information and his recreation, his love and his religion. He hardly kno
him, he's always doing both." —James A. Michener "We are what we continually do. Excellence therefore is not an act, bt
ou are." —Theodore Roosevelt "That's a BB in a boxcar." —William H. Harrison "The woods are lovely, dark and deep,
l 90% how you respond to it." —Bill's Grandmother Harrison "There are dreamers, but not all human beings dream equal
reamers of the Day are dangerous people because they act their dreams into reality with open eyes." —T.E. Lawrence "The
n and his recreation, his love and his religion. He hardly knows which is which. He simply pursues his vision of excellence a
hat we continually do. Excellence therefore is not an act, but a habit." —Aristotle "In the land of the blind, the one-eyed m
—William H. Harrison "The woods are lovely, dark and deep, but I have promises to keep, and miles to go before I sleep
son "There are dreamers, but not all human beings dream equally. Some are dreamers of the night, who in the dusty recesse
eir dreams into reality with open eyes." —T.E. Lawrence "The master in the art of living makes little distinction between h
nows which is which. He simply pursues his vision of excellence at whatever he does, leaving others to decide whether he is
but a habit." —Aristotle "In the land of the blind, the one-eyed man is king." —Desiderius Erasmus "Do what you can w
leep, but I have promises to keep, and miles to go before I sleep, and miles to go before I sleep." —Robert Frost "Life is 10
n equally. Some are dreamers of the night, who in the dusty recesses of their mind, dream and wake in the morning to find
"The master in the art of living makes little distinction between his work and his play, his labor and his leisure, his mind a
cellence at whatever he does, leaving others to decide whether he is working or playing. To him, he's always doing both." —
ne-eyed man is king." —Desiderius Erasmus "Do what you can with what you have where you are." —Theodore Roosevelt
leep, and miles to go before I sleep." —Robert Frost "Life is 10% what happens to you and 90% how you respond to it." —
e recesses of their mind, dream and wake in the morning to find it was just vanity. But the Dreamers of the Day are dangero
ween his work and his play, his labor and his leisure, his mind and his body, his information and his recreation, his love ar
ther he is working or playing. To him, he's always doing both." —James A. Michener "We are what we continually do. Exc
you can with what you have where you are." —Theodore Roosevelt "That's a BB in a boxcar." —William H. Harrison "T
Life is 10% what happens to you and 90% how you respond to it." —Bill's Grandmother Harrison "There are dreamers, b
o find it was just vanity. But the Dreamers of the Day are dangerous people because they act their dreams into reality with
, his mind and his body, his information and his recreation, his love and his religion. He hardly knows which is which. He
g both." —James A. Michener "We are what we continually do. Excellence therefore is not an act, but a habit." —Aristot
e Roosevelt "That's a BB in a boxcar." —William H. Harrison "The woods are lovely, dark and deep, but I have promises
pond to it." —Bill's Grandmother Harrison "There are dreamers, but not all human beings dream equally. Some are dream
re dangerous people because they act their dreams into reality with open eyes." —T.E. Lawrence "The master in the art of
on, his love and his religion. He hardly knows which is which. He simply pursues his vision of excellence at whatever he do
do. Excellence therefore is not an act, but a habit." —Aristotle "In the land of the blind, the one-eyed man is king." —D
son "The woods are lovely, dark and deep, but I have promises to keep, and miles to go before I sleep, and miles to go befo
dreamers, but not all human beings dream equally. Some are dreamers of the night, who in the dusty recesses of their mind
o reality with open eyes." —T.E. Lawrence "The master in the art of living makes little distinction between his work and h
which. He simply pursues his vision of excellence at whatever he does, leaving others to decide whether he is working or p
-Aristotle "In the land of the blind, the one-eyed man is king." —Desiderius Erasmus "Do what you can with what you ha
romises to keep, and miles to go before I sleep, and miles to go before I sleep." —Robert Frost "Life is 10% what happen
re dreamers of the night, who in the dusty recesses of their mind, dream and wake in the morning to find it was just vanity
the art of living makes little distinction between his work and his play, his labor and his leisure, his mind and his body, his

25

HARRISON
DESIGN

Harrison Design is an Atlanta-based architecture firm with deep southern roots that reach a national and an increasing international clientele. By 2016, with projects around the world, the firm's success story, chronicled here in this celebratory retrospective, has at its core the ever-present commitment, whole-hearted curiosity, intuition, and fearlessness in the energetic form of founder, William H. Harrison.

This book celebrates twenty-five years of architectural design services, the clients and patrons who have commissioned thousands of projects, the allied services and craftspeople, and the roster of talented staff along the way. The firm's development, range, and consideration of the future is illustrated pictorially along with personal histories of those in leadership today. Foremost, the book is about people and the relationships, trust, and patience that allow for the interpretation of dreams.

PLATE 1

PLATE 2

CONTACT HARRISON DESIGN
3198 Cains Hill Place NW, Atlanta, GA 30305

ISBN 978-1-5323-0471-2
LIBRARY OF CONGRESS CONTROL NUMBER 2016948343
FIRST EDITION

WRITER
Henrika Dyck Taylor

EDITORIAL
Joni Emerson Diehl, Lee Brooks Kinsella, Henrika Dyck Taylor

DESIGNER
Dyad Communications
Philadelphia, Pennsylvania

PRINTER
Crystal World Printing
Manufactured in China

FRONT JACKET IMAGE
The jacket cover image is reproduced with gracious permission and courtesy
of iStar Financial and the Mandarin Oriental. Photograph by Mali Azima.

BACK JACKET IMAGE
Photograph by Lauren Rubinstein.

Harrison Design has supplied all information and illustrations for this publication. Every effort has been
made to ensure accuracy and credit the original source of copyright material contained in this book. Project
photography is credited in the Image Index (pp. 446-449). Drawings, renderings, and archival photographs
are used by permission of Harrison Design. Additional photography is by Peter Olson unless otherwise noted.
Contact Harrison Design directly to rectify any errors or omissions.

Contents

"There are dreamers, but not all human beings dream equally. Some are dreamers of the night, who in the dusty recesses of their mind, dream and wake in the morning to find it was just vanity. But the Dreamers of the Day are dangerous people because they act their dreams into reality with open eyes."

—T. E. LAWRENCE, SEVEN PILLARS OF WISDOM

TO OUR CLIENTS

Your dreams have given wings to our passion
and purpose to our practice.

Thank you.

PLATE 3

Foreword

Dedicated to the clients of Harrison Design, this monograph celebrates the collaboration that produces architecture. The luscious photographs of built work and the personal stories of the firm's associates chronicle the making of beautiful places. These multiple voices redress a void in the literature of the profession by their representation of the team effort, too often concealed by focus on the practice leader. The stories show people who love their work. The photos show the results of the care and joy of that work.

This acknowledgement of the workaday world of architecture, the variety of people and skills combined with the time needed to produce places, is a reminder that architecture builds civilizations. It is the physical manifestation of culture, the shared values and aspirations of a people and a time.

Harrison Design's dedication to traditional architecture, to advancing the knowledge and achievements of predecessors, connects not only with the precedents but also with their generating aspirations. By such an engagement with history, classical architecture came to represent the aspirations of the early nineteenth century South. Today, a new generation draws upon the best of their foregoers, to continue the traditions that are our architectural heritage.

That this heritage is carried on most evidently in residential building is appropriate as the house is the sacred territory of our country like no other. Individual clients thus are enabled as patrons of the culture. They are participants in full, from initiative to inhabitation, pursuing excellence as backdrop for the pursuit of happiness. And what a rich experience, living with graceful details that record a craftsman's clever and exact solution to a problem, integrated with contemporary technologies.

There are those who will question such an endeavor, claiming that the wrongs of an era should prohibit its emulation — that it is complicit with the injustice to engage the aesthetic attached to the times. But our own period of the modern can certainly compete with the perfidies of the past. And the hubris of erasing history no matter how often undertaken, always disappoints. This focus on tradition is one of learning from it and reclaiming the good of it.

Harrison Design already has developed its own history. The record of twenty-five years shows the process of the profession's re-acquaintance with its heritage, after the modernist negation. It was only at the third quarter of the twentieth century that architects once again felt free to roam the halls of history, in travel, in books, and in design. The tentative references of Post-Modernism enabled the return to the authentic.

In Harrison Design's work one sees the return to the authentic: highly evolved, demanding of craftsmanship, engaging not only the European traditions, but also the vernacular buildings of the pioneering rural settlement of the West, and as well, our newest tradition, the modern. A portfolio that combines orthodox emulation as well as contemporary invention requires versatility of skill, and recalls the last great generation of Beaux Arts trained architects who negotiated both.

Across this range of design language, is evident a pattern and continuum of production. The reader will find that the personal trajectories often began with knowledge gained in study, then took on making in construction, and later traveled to touch the history. The importance of hand drawings, sketches and detail studies is emphasized, a creative process that parallels the craft of production. And ultimately, the constructed result that revels in details, hand-made as well as machined, sharing tried and true experience in form and firmness. All support, as Bill says, the ultimate benchmark of excellence — the test of time.

For recognizing his clients' desire to contribute to this history, for his ambition to bring it into the present and future, and for his skill in assembling and managing the cadre of dedicated designers and builders, Bill Harrison deserves admiration. Bill's initiative and wisdom in developing a design-build operation into a sophisticated award-winning architectural practice, and his resilience, finding advantage in difficult economic times, is a lesson for architects of any persuasion.

Bill's entrepreneurial skill emerged from his early engagement with construction, and from his youthful experience in other arenas at a time when the values of social justice and environmental responsibility were emerging. These have guided his business practices ever since. Besides illustrating his integrity, the story of his early experiences hint at the potential for an entertaining autobiography! The stories of his associates tell us that he encourages for them the same individual growth that he experienced.

The firm's commitment to service and philanthropy are a reflection of Bill's generosity. Bill's service on the Board of Directors of the Institute of Classical Architecture and Art (ICAA), and the funding and personal time contributed to Georgia Tech and the University of Miami, reflects the goal shared with his associates, to support the knowledge and practice of classical and traditional architecture, in particular for students.

The pages ahead invite exploration in many ways and more than once. The architect will see them as a mother-lode of contemporary experience to be mined. Others will delight in the visual and the personal stories. Whether in sequence or by ad hoc forays, the reader is certain to enjoy getting to know the work of Harrison Design.

ELIZABETH PLATER-ZYBERK, *August 2016*

PLATE 4

PLATE 5

PLATE 6

PLATE 7

1

BEGINNINGS

William H. Harrison

"We are what we continually do. Excellence therefore is not an act, but a habit." —Aristotle

Harrison Design, formerly Harrison Design Associates, began in the 1970s as a company called Harrison Construction. Harrison Construction quickly evolved into a thriving design-build enterprise as William H. Harrison, known as Bill to everyone, established his client base first in Atlanta and then throughout the southeast. Twenty-five years after dedicating his firm to the art of residential architecture, Bill and his colleagues are preparing a long view towards what comes next.

But this story begins much earlier.

Originally from Macon, Georgia, Bill worked as a draftsman for a local architect while still in high school, and later attended Georgia Institute of Technology to study architecture. His earliest ambitions, however, were not as linear as one might think. At the age of twelve Bill was considering his options. Along with architecture, his short list of interests included nuclear physics, ballet, and neurosurgery. Ultimately, because he liked to draw, he decided to investigate architecture.

Resourceful and determined, Bill got out the yellow pages and looked up architects in his hometown. He found Hank Dixon who liked Bill's youthful drawings and attitude. So on weekends and during the summers for several years, Hank mentored Bill. He taught him basic drafting and how to letter and gave him tasks on real projects. Today Bill credits Hank Dixon for making a difference in his life and guiding him in more than just his profession.

Dixon's abiding example of kindness, being of service, and "telling it like it is" are characteristics Bill embodies today.

Bill's early focus served him well as he began his academic career at Georgia Tech's School of Architecture. He was a good student and he acknowledges his supportive family for instilling his innate curiosity. In addition to his schoolwork, where he had a drafting skill advantage over many of the students due to his head start with Hank Dixon, Bill worked loading UPS trucks at night to help pay his way. He worked

very hard, determined to be the best worker they had, but was fired for loading the trucks too efficiently! The UPS Human Resources department recognized his efforts and potential: They gave him a generous severance and recommended that he start his own business and only work for himself. The severance and words of advice became the start up money and impetus that started Bill on his entrepreneurial way.

His inaugural business venture engaged class-mates as associates. Bill marshaled the students to produce models and renderings for local architecture businesses. Bill solicited and managed the work, collected timesheets, and did the accounting. He paid his young colleagues well and kept a small percentage for organizing the enterprise. All the while, through his freshman and sophomore years, Bill was a classic over-achiever, maintaining high grades, serving as class president and social chairman of his fraternity (which included as a member William Mitchell, who became the renowned Atlanta-based architecture historian).

In Bill's words, "All this activity was interesting, but I became tapped out and restless." So in 1969, with the savings from his architectural model business, he checked out of school and headed to California. During his trek west, whether by luck, courage, or willful abandon, Bill managed time and time again to land on his feet. In short order, he found himself working for Richard C. Peters, then the Dean of the School of Architecture at the University of California, Berkeley, whose firm was known for its groundbreaking work in lighting design.

In those days, the hippy movement was prevalent in Berkeley after all, and Bill joined the counter culture. Eventually, he made his way back across the country and re-enrolled at Georgia Tech. With his long hair and recent more worldly experiences, however, he was not the same Mr. College persona from his freshman and sophomore years. He began hanging out in the district of Atlanta where leather crafts and tooling were in demand. His ability to sew (his mother taught him years before) prepared him well for creating belts and jackets and he soon developed a following.

Originally, Bill's leather business was all custom work, but over time, he hired a tailor and employees to keep up with his eager customers. As his company began making stock and selling to stores, brand name corporations discovered Bill's leather apparel. Genesco, a national leather goods outfit based in Nashville, ordered thousands of belts in a month. Bill didn't say no, but his friends and workers were already making them as fast as possible on the kitchen table and it was clear they wouldn't make the deadline. Enter Lovable Company, a local lingerie establishment, which was struggling to stay afloat. At that particular time in history, foundation garments were not at all in vogue, so the company rented its factory and garment production equipment to Bill and the belts were produced to meet the big demand month after month. To maintain this effort, Bill also hired the men who worked in Atlanta's shoe repair shops, and then bought out the shops.

Billy Harrison
Sophomore Representative Student Council; Member IFC Rush Book Committee; First, Second Vice President, and President Triangle Club; Chairman Community Service Committee; YMCA Cabinet; American Institute of Architects; T-Book Staff.

By late-1970, Bill was managing a wholesale leather business and was doing custom feather and beadwork. While he created clothing and accessories—bags, belts, fringed vests, jackets, and halter-tops—that defined the 70s generation, ventures in the nightclub and entertainment industry naturally followed suit. Bill became part of a partnership that managed live events in clubs and theatres around the country. The Great Music Hall in Atlanta presented acts like Pure Prairie

League, Johnny Cash, Willie Nelson, Dolly Parton, and John Prine among others. Similarly, acts were booked at the Bottom Line and Filmore East in New York, and Filmore West in San Francisco.

During all this, while having an enormous number of people working for him, Bill finished his thesis in architecture. For nearly two years after earning his degree, he retained an unrelenting pace, motivating and invigorating those around him while he managed his leather goods factory and retail stores as well as his partnerships in the entertainment business. Fun and success notwithstanding, Bill knew he was not fulfilling his real purpose in life.

Thus, with characteristic decisiveness, Bill sold his manufacturing operation and his share of the entertainment business. The shoe repair shops he sold to men who had originally worked there and who had become loyal employees and businessmen under Bill's mentorship. Two of these establishments remain in business today.

After the sale of his businesses, Bill had plenty of money to support himself and read plenty of books before embarking on his next endeavor. Sparked in particular by reading *Sailing Around the World*—a true account of a solo adventure written in 1899 by Joshua Slocum—Bill determined that he would buy a boat, learn to sail, and have his own trans-Atlantic experience. In the Chesapeake Bay, he found a 42-foot wooden ketch that was built in 1957. He spent nearly a year getting the boat and himself seaworthy. He learned how to sail, dock, and handle his boat, and he taught himself how to navigate with a sextant.

When he and his boat, *The Osprey*, were ready, Bill sailed down the east coast to Central and South America via the Caribbean and from there made his way to England, France, the Mediterranean, and Venice. Suffice it to say that the tale of Bill's sailing adventure and European sojourn is another story for another book. While Bill traveled, he found himself considering the architecture with renewed interest and often worked with various artisans along the way. While in the Veneto region, he systematically visited all of Andrea Palladio's villas and spent months in Italy studying and drawing before heading home via the Azores. He had roamed around Europe for two years and the experience buttressed his intellect, resilience, and curiosity. He sailed home thus fortified, ready to resume his trajectory as an architect.

Back in Atlanta and impassioned anew about building and architecture from his journey, Bill began to buy up derelict houses near Inman Park in a mill village called Cabbagetown, which was listed on the National Register of Historic Places. He renovated two-story shotgun houses and cottages with roofers and masons and millworkers, and promptly sold them as the area became popular again. He also bought an old brick building (919 Wylie Street SE) in Reynoldstown, another historic district adjacent to Cabbagetown. Bill's building, which pre-dated the Civil War, had been used as a hospital so was spared during the 1864 destruction of Atlanta. Bill lived and worked from this building while teaching himself the construction business. It was during this time that Bill began to engage, train, and encourage local craftspeople; many of them continue to work with his architecture firm today.

During the 1980s, the region in and around Atlanta was known for its conservative climate for new architecture, but the Cabbagetown renovations, restorations, and refurbishments that fueled Bill's construction business provided entrée to a customer base. As Bill reflects, "I was from Macon and although I attended Georgia Tech, I had no other claim to Atlanta other than I wanted to make my home and career there. I knew no one and relied on word of mouth for referrals."

Bill says of his fearlessness when it comes to taking risks, "My dad was entrepreneurial so his successful enterprises were what I observed and knew. My mother, brother, sisters, and other relatives all set the example of 'when a door opens, go for it.' Listen to everyone and learn from everything. Distill the essence."

MIROSLAWA L. IRLIK
A Profile in Commitment

IN AUGUST 1987, Miroslawa L. Irlik responded to a job posting in the *Atlanta Journal-Constitution* newspaper for a company called Harrison Construction. The available position was for a residential architect. Mira, as she is known, had eight years of architectural experience in Poland and had just immigrated to America. She was captivated by the architecture of the estate homes around Atlanta—the gracious porticoes, arches, and gables—which were so different than what she knew from her home country. Prior to her arrival, Mira also spent some time in Madrid, where that city's iconic architecture and history opened her eyes to something very new. She was 27 years old, barely spoke English, and was determined to find a job in architecture so she could continue to grow in her chosen profession. She wanted to learn how to create harmonious, beautiful architecture that would be a pleasure to live in. The job description for an architect to work on high-end residential projects sparked her imagination and "new calling" in architecture.

Of course in those days, there was no Internet to research, no website, and none of Harrison Design's books had been published yet. There was no way to know anything about the company.

Nonetheless, Mira took a bus to the Cabbagetown neighborhood for her interview with Harrison Construction, and almost turned back

as she observed blocks of ramshackle shotgun houses in a district that didn't seem safe. When she arrived at the best house on Wylie Street, she still wasn't sure about the logistics of commuting to that part of town, but was intrigued by the lovely building, which had huge floor to ceiling double-hung windows.

She recalls, "The entry was also nice so I was encouraged and thought at the least I could practice my interview skills. My English was pretty sketchy though and my conversation with Bill Harrison did not go very well." Mira's previous experience had been on commercial buildings, libraries, stadiums, and condominiums. Houses at that time in Poland were very modern and built of concrete and not at all like the houses that Harrison was doing for his clients. She was dismissed.

But Mira held her ground. By that point, she decided that she wanted the job in spite of the iffy commute and wanted to work for Bill. She saw her chance to work on the kinds of houses she revered and wanted to learn from Bill. Poland didn't have such a thing as "high-end residential" architecture. It was too poor a country, but she had worked on huge difficult commissions, had the experience, and knew she could handle houses, so she gathered her courage, tried again, and persuaded Bill to hire her.

Initially, Mira liaised with interior designer Susan Reinstein who found Mira dedicated, quick, and capable indeed. A month later, as a very large estate project was on the boards, Bill needed help and Mira proved to be indispensible. As she says, "My hard work and Bill's creativity made us an inseparable team." This first project they completed together was 35,000 square feet and Mira did all the drawings. During this venture, with Bill's support, Mira pioneered telecommuting, working from home while her sons were small. The estate, called Dean Gardens, was completed in 1989 and gave the company terrific exposure that contributed to the firm's purely architectural focus a few years later.

In 2016, Mira is still with Harrison Design and has the distinction of having the firm's longest employment. She fell in love with the work and found that it filled a gap in her modernist education at the Politechnika Slaska-Gliwice (Silesian University of Technology).

Growing up in Poland Mira watched as her country recreated its infrastructure and wanted to somehow play a part in its progress. "I wanted to contribute towards the new community planning that was so needed in my country. I thought I would design nice places for families to live and work and I wanted a job that would become a career."

Mira did not want to leave Poland, but life there in the mid-1980s became untenable and her family made the decision to leave. No easy feat, but resolve, circumstances, and the kindness of strangers landed her in Atlanta. Mira fully embraced her new environment, reimagined her professional

calling, and raised her children.

The hand drawing, design, plan development, and history of architecture from her education ended up playing a role in the interior architecture work she now loves to do most. "Embellishing a room to make it come alive with architecture is hugely satisfying. Cabinetry, paneling, bookcases, crown mouldings, lighting—I am infatuated by ceilings in particular. I have come full circle back to what Susan inspired in me over twenty-five years ago."

About Bill and why she continues at Harrison Design Mira says, "I love the work, but it is also how Bill treats people. I saw firsthand over all the years how Bill thought about his staff and mentored us all. We are encouraged to be independent and our ideas and creativity matter. He believes that our being hands-on is better for our professional development and in turn is better for the clients."

Mira continues, "Opportunities are given here. If you want to do something it is acknowledged. Bill has a knack for choosing people. We have different backgrounds, different nationalities, and different experiences. His interest and curiosity about people is boundless. Everyone has a place to belong and contribute and it is a privilege to play a part. Sure, now and then things don't work out and certainly there are disagreements, but everyone has a voice. We have the option to speak up and air our opinions as long as we are open to a discussion."

Mira concludes, "As a result of Bill's strong spirit and leadership the firm has accomplished so much. It has made careers for so many. It made a lot of clients happy. It has given back to many organizations and institutions. It continues to shape lives. I can honestly say I love to go to work every day."

"GRACE PERSONIFIED. She is a fire-walker, yet carries herself with such elegance I think she must have been royalty in another life."

—BILL HARRISON, 2016

Sometimes opportunities took Bill in a new direction altogether. Other times, talented people joined forces with Bill to take his pursuits to the next level. By 1989, Bill's construction enterprise engaged scores of hourly employees. That same year, Deborah Harrison left the world of mergers and acquisitions to take on the financial development and oversight of the burgeoning, if unwieldy, business. Her brilliant management and vision of Harrison Construction allowed Bill to focus on design-build and architecture, which led him to open Harrison Design Associates in 1991 as a full-fledged architectural services firm.

Between 1991 and 1995, Bill's particular brand of ingenuity and gregariousness began to attract larger and more complex commissions, and he and his then small drafting staff were working in response to an increased demand for his design expertise. Clients were often self-made entrepreneurs and innovators who were drawn to Bill and the artistry he and his firm could provide. In 1995, architect Greg Palmer was hired. The roster of clients had blossomed and Greg had the residential experience and presence the firm needed along with a unique knack for leading numbers of people to a cohesive, successful conclusion. He and Bill subsequently mentored a Georgia Tech architecture graduate named Bulent Baydar, who was hired the same year.

The team stayed pretty much the same, along with Miroslawa L. Irlik (who has worked with Bill since 1987) until 1998 when Bill and Greg hired architects and designers Rick Hatch, John Albanese, Chad Goehring, Derek Hopkins, and Robbie Pich; controller Carol Hayes; and interior designer Karen

Ferguson, many of whom, among others who came later, are the next generation of leadership at Harrison Design.

With this new talent and some favorable press, a buzz grew in Atlanta due to the completion of several large estate projects and by 2000 Harrison Design had taken on a large percentage of the traditional residential market in Buckhead. Recognizing that further growth to sustain the firm would not be possible close to home, Bill began to look further afield. An opportunity developed when *Traditional Home* magazine commissioned the firm to design and build a show house in Santa Barbara, California, which proved to be a wonderful opening for the firm's presence on the west coast. Consequently, in 2004, Harrison Design merged with Santa Barbara architect Tony Spann to create what continues to be an ongoing success.

In 2006, the St. Simons office opened to serve clients in southeastern coastal communities. Then, in response to what became an eighteen-month recession, Harrison Design opened offices in Los Angeles, Washington, DC, and New York, which served regions less affected by the economic downturn. First, in 2007, based on the solid footing and reputation won in Santa Barbara, the Los Angeles office opened in Beverly Hills on Wilshire Boulevard, which by 2013 relocated to Century City. In 2008, the firm also added projects in China and the Middle East.

"Listen to everyone and learn from everything. Distill the essence."

The Washington, DC office was a natural addition in 2010 following the *Southern Accents* McLean, Virginia show house, which had steadily generated business in that region. A New York office emerged in 2011 and like the other Harrison Design satellites, became an extension of the firm as a direct result of Bill's "when-a door-opens" spirit and personality.

By diversifying the office markets, and adding a Landscape Architecture studio at the Atlanta office, Harrison Design demonstrated time and again that it was able to withstand regional economic declines and stylistic trends. A full-fledged national organization in 2016, the Atlanta office and its studios offer constant support to the other locations. The close contact among principals and project architects reinforces their resources and camaraderie.

As the firm celebrates its twenty-fifth anniversary, Bill is increasingly interested in mentoring the next generation. He says, "I like to design and I'm always ready for the next project. I am endlessly curious about people. My staff and my clients inspired me to get through six recessions. I tell people, 'Get out and do. Get over your fears, get out of your own way and figure it out.' I want to give back to the industry by talking about my experiences, the firm's work, and the importance of relationships."

Bill continues, "If I have learned anything from my path, it is to invest in people. I have come back to this basic truth again and again. At one point when we

had a huge office, I had to make choices about what was most important. I chose to focus on residential architecture, hired creative people who could have—and did have—their own offices, but who wished to work as part of a larger establishment. They benefit from the back office and personnel support from the main Atlanta office. We have a deep synergy and the increasing quality of the work is a result."

Ruminating over how his clients found him in the past and now, Bill credits his willingness to listen, the firm's unwavering standards for materials and work-manship, and commitment to deliver. Happy clients simply spread the word. He says, "For me, creating

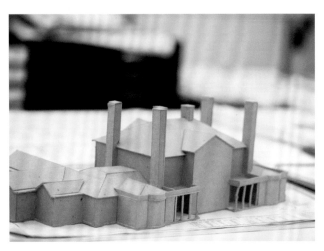

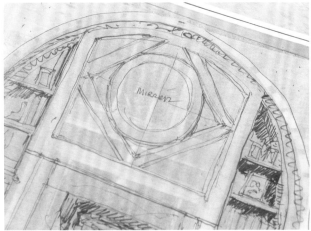

architecture for our clients has never been about a particular style, it is about the best design and best building we can provide based on our clients' wishes. It is a privilege to gain the trust and confidence required to create something wonderful. We have had the good fortune to have the appropriate skill and talent on board to contribute to the success of any project, regardless of the desired outcome. In the end, that is the joy and why we keep doing it."

In her 1994 article about Bill Harrison, "Details make the Difference," Rachel Canfield quotes Bill regarding his principles thusly: He said, "If you build it, it could be there forever. Why not build it right? You've got to have good design and good execution of the design—the people building it are more important than I am. Create something that will survive the client and the generations to follow…The judge of good architecture: Does it stand the test of time?"

In 2016, Bill's fundamental principles about architecture and building have not wavered. The senior staff and principals at Harrison Design are mentoring the next wave of talent to carry on the firm's studio system. Creating a close-knit staff across the studios and departments is crucial to the success of the work and critical to the firm's ongoing appeal.

Refined work, from the largest project to the most modest, is hard won with skill, long hours, flexibility, and above all a willingness to serve. Bill sets this resolute example and holds everyone accountable. He says, "I am proud of what has been accomplished and what we have increasingly in place to continue doing great work. It is really about the people and letting them grow into themselves just as I did."

In 2013, Bill Harrison was honored by the Southeast Chapter of the Institute of Classical Architecture & Art (ICAA) with the inaugural "Medal of Vesta," which acknowledged him as "the keeper of the eternal flame" for his commitment to architectural education. Deeply moved, Bill said in his acceptance speech, "After school, when I traveled in Italy and saw the villas of Palladio for the very first time, it was the most enlightening moment of my life to see such perfect spaces. Years later, when my firm became successful, I began to think about that defining opportunity, which basically happened to me by accident. It overwhelmed me. What if students of architecture today and beyond don't have such an opportunity, by accident or otherwise? How can I contribute to make sure that this critical component in any designers' path is guaranteed? How can I be part of a solution? How can the architects that come behind us learn to see in a different way? How can the principles of beauty be part of architectural curricula? These are the questions that galvanize me daily. I continue to ask these questions while supporting leaders and educators in architecture. It is our collective task as practitioners, educators, and patrons alike to remember to take our successes beyond ourselves. It is my duty, with all of you, to lay the path to the future."

PLATE 8

PLATE 9

PLATE 10

PLATE II

PLATE 12

PLATE 13

PLATE 14

PLATES 15–16

PLATE 17

DEBORAH H. HARRISON
A Tribute

DEBORAH HARRISON'S contributions to the development and growth of Harrison Design cannot be overstated. As the finance and business manager since 1989, and principal until her retirement from day to day management in 2016, Deborah thoughtfully guided the firm through each phase of its evolution and prepared wisely for its expansion along the way. Her long-term planning accords Harrison Design a constant path forward.

An industrial engineer by training and an MBA with background in corporate investments and the building industry, Deborah systematized processes to run the business more effectively. She routinely sought and implemented ways to enrich employees' involvement and rewards. Productivity comes from happy people, and Deborah's hands-on approach and regular evaluation of standards made sure that everyone had appropriate and generous benefits. She worked tirelessly to improve the work environment for all.

During the firm's design-build days, the company had a myriad of independent contractors and tabulation of timesheets and billing was an overwhelming chore. Deborah created a unique online financial system that allowed for efficiency and completely overhauled the business model and its practices. Today, her innovations in financial tracking allow project architects across the country to stay on top of their clients' budgets. She also built a skilled finance corps, members of which have been with the firm for decades.

Deborah's exactitude, expertise, and presence allowed Founder, Bill Harrison and Senior Principal, Greg Palmer the freedom to develop their artistry and leadership. Likewise, Deborah took care of Harrison Design's staff, designers, and architects so all could do their work to the best of their ability.

Her passion for sustainability and stewardship of the natural environment led to the firm's philanthropic activity with Atlanta's Fernbank Museum of Natural History. Deborah thusly established a model for the architectural leaders, who share her heart and resolve as they further the

firm's philanthropy within arts and education.

On the cusp of the company's twenty-fifth anniversary, Harrison Design gratefully acknowledges Deborah Harrison for establishing its financial and business framework; for creating methodologies to attract and retain the finest talent; and for personally shaping the firm's core twin values of philanthropy and service.

PLATE 18

PLATES 19-22

PLATE 23

PLATE 24

PLATE 25

PLATE 26

59

PLATE 27

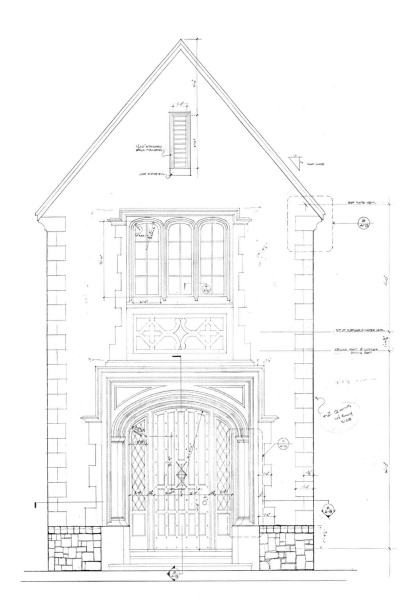

61

PLATE 28

PLATE 29

PLATE 30

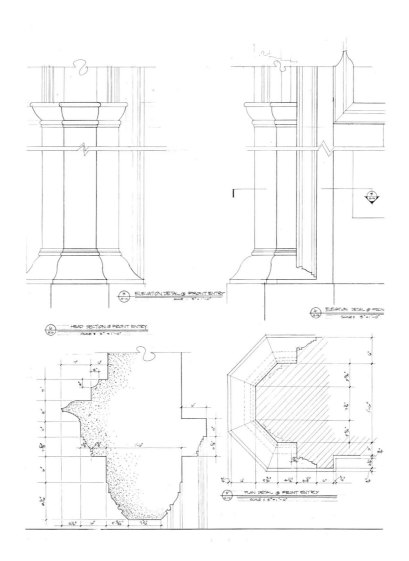

ELEVATION DETAIL @ FRONT ENTRY
SCALE : 3" = 1'-0"

ELEVATION DETAIL @ FRONT
SCALE : 3" = 1'-0"

HEAD SECTION @ FRONT ENTRY
SCALE : 3" = 1'-0"

PLAN DETAIL @ FRONT ENTRY
SCALE : 3" = 1'-0"

PLATES 31–32

PLATE 33

PLATE 34

2

EARLY GROWTH

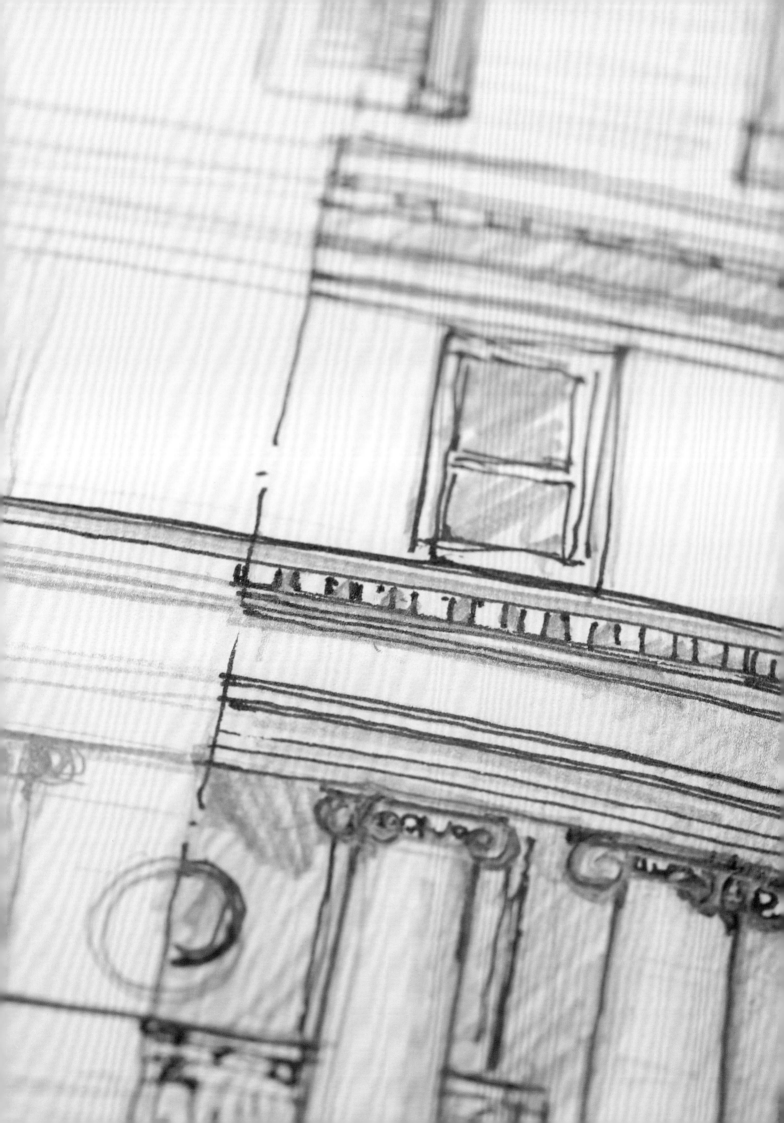

Gregory L. Palmer

Building a Practice

Gregory L. Palmer is Harrison Design's most senior architecture principal; he embodies the spirit of the firm not only as a sought-after designer, but also as a gifted manager who retains near-flawless memory of people, names, places, and dates. As such, Greg is the natural keeper of the institutional history, both before and since his arrival at Harrison Design Associates in 1995. Along with Bill Harrison, he also is a logical-minded proponent for leading the Harrison Design philosophy and vision into the future.

When Greg joined Bill and the small crew at Harrison Design Associates (or HDA as the firm was known then), he was a recent graduate of Southern Technical Institute and had just passed his architecture licensing exams. Greg's first-hand experience in his family's second generation-run general contracting business led to a keen interest in construction and residential architecture and motivated him to become both a licensed architect and building contractor. He recalls, "The summer I was sixteen, I was in a hole digging a foundation in the blistering South Georgia heat when the architect for the project arrived on the site. He embodied respect with his knowledge and ability and he looked the part, Panama hat and all. It was a defining moment for me and right then I knew what I wanted to do with my life."

Prior to his arrival at HDA, Greg interned with a respected Atlanta firm where he worked on the design and production of large estate projects. Likewise, Greg's impassioned dedication to studying and drawing from the Renaissance masters—Michelangelo and Andrea Palladio in particular—as well as eighteenth- and nineteenth-century architects Sir Christopher Wren and Sir Edwin Lutyens among others, made him an ideal colleague and eventual shareholder at Harrison Design Associates.

Within two years of Greg's arrival, he and Bill had assembled a small group of dedicated personnel and completed several large and noteworthy regional projects. These projects established HDA as

a contender in the local traditional architecture market. At the same time, Greg established leadership and management practices that not only nurtured the core talent then on board, but that attracted first-rate and forthcoming practitioners to the office.

Greg recalls, "It was exciting to see the level of work we were producing then and the commissions kept coming, each one providing an opportunity for us to stretch and grow. For me personally, by the time I was in my mid-thirties, I was working on an extraordinary residential project. The design for this 30,000-square-foot mansion was hand-drawn in sixty days and it took five years to build. It was a wildly complex program that demanded the most beautiful materials and the highest caliber of craftsmanship in the world. The experience was the crucible that gave me incredible confidence and faith in myself."

Greg continues, "At Harrison Design everyone feels a level of owner-ship and has the desire to keep the bar high. I think people stay because their contributions matter. It is a professional environ-ment, it is a business, and we are a family. We are in it together. Bill creates this context, along with his passion for our craft, from which we all have benefited. Architects and long-time staff members like Mira Irlik, Bulent Baydar, Rick Hatch, John Albanese, Chad Goehring, Tony Spann, and others have stepped up in so many ways and emerged as part of our current leadership. They are guiding the next generation."

Greg continues, "As early as 1999-2000, we be-gan to have long discussions about succession plans and what was important to us as a firm." By then Harrison Design Associates had raised its profile and was doing very well. Greg and Bill were asking themselves and others tough questions about focus, vision, and what they wished to instill in younger practitioners who were poised to become the next generation of HDA principals. They determined that Harrison Design would aspire to two goals: 1) Retain and continue to improve the firm's viability and skill in the national residential marketplace, and 2) Give back to the communities in which their of-fices were located to reflect the company's ideals and individual passions."

"IT IS HUGELY SATISFYING ALL THESE YEARS LATER TO SEE HOW THE CURRENT STAFF EMBODIES THE FOUNDATIONAL ETHOS THAT DEVELOPED SO ORGANICALLY IN THE EARLY YEARS OF THE FIRM."

One such example of the firm's service stems from Greg and Bill's shared passion for affect-ing change in the way ar-chitecture is taught in the United States. They have steered a deliberate effort to influence architecture curricula in universities open to teaching the te-nets of classicism. The firm's support at Geor-gia Tech led to the creation of the Harrison Design Associates Visiting Scholar and a Master of Science degree in classical design was also piloted as a direct result. Another example is the firm's encouragement of active participation on boards of local and nation-al organizations, including the Institute of Classical Architecture & Art (ICAA). Since its inception, the Atlanta-based ICAA Southeast Chapter—founded in 2004 and one of the first regional ICAA chap-ters established—continues to set a precedent with

educational offerings and its trailblazing regional awards program, the Philip Trammell Shutze
Awards. In 2016, Greg is serving as the Southeast
Chapter's president, which underscores his personal
dedication and leadership.

By 2004, a new balance in responsibility was forged
to further broaden the firm's presence. Greg took on
a larger role in sales and marketing, which previously
had been Bill's domain. In the ensuing years, Greg
also provided hands-on support for the St. Simons,
Georgia and Washington, DC offices, keeping up a
fierce travel schedule that included regular junkets
to China and the Middle East as projects developed
there. "An increase in exceptional staff since the mid-
2000s and a well-established atelier system allows
the firm to retain quality and pace." Greg continues,
"Our studios are mutually supportive, efficient, and
objective. They are at the root of our success, allow-
ing us to address regional and cultural differences,
and to be nimble across the stylistic desires of our
clients."

Considering where the firm is now, Greg notes,
"In 2016, we are blessed to have better work than
ever. Not bigger, or more expensive, but better.
Our clients have become very savvy thanks to the
Internet. Over the years, we found contractors and
builders with whom we have established a common
language and understanding. Great design is only as
good as its built execution and we have a strong net-
work of people who can build to our specifications
and standards."

To Greg, it is a hopeful time. The firm navigated
through economic downturns and survived not only

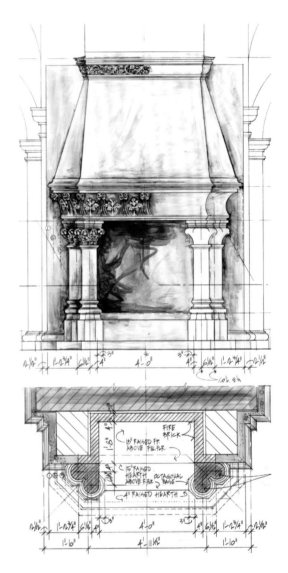

intact, but also more dedicated than ever. "Getting through those hard times drives us to stay on top of the profession, which has changed so dramatically in twenty-five years. The change keeps it interesting. Never rest on what reputation comes before you. Bill's design strength and salesmanship propelled us down the road, hiring good associates got us even further, and I am eager to see what comes next."

"Meanwhile," Greg cautions with a nod to the future, "more than ever, drawing by hand is essential. It still communicates what technology cannot and enhances what technology does so well." Greg sketches a lot, as do most in the firm, which is a boon when demonstrating ideas and solutions to clients and staff alike. "Travel has also played a huge part in my own development as an architect and as a person. My first trip abroad was to Monaco and the South of France. There is no substitution for the personal experience of 'seeing' first hand what I'd studied and read about for so long. Taking the time to experience other places, to slow down and really look at architecture and building traditions past and present is hugely inspir-

ing and contributes to fluency and invention in my designs. Along that vein, in terms of slowing down and striking a balance, I would also advise anyone in our field to trust in themselves, take the risks, and spend more time with your children. You don't get the time back."

As Greg reflects on what has most influenced his career at Harrison Design, he says, "For me, it is the synthesis of relationships; I care so much about getting to know our clients. To play a part in their lives is priceless. Gaining their trust to embark on what is likely the single most expensive investment of their lives is equal to watching the growth and success of our people. I love to observe natural strengths in an individual and optimize his or her abilities within the context of a studio. It is a thrill to see confidence and skill manifest in the myriad details of a project and in the emerging leadership of the firm."

Greg concludes, "Observing Harrison Design's anniversary allows for a rare moment to consider how far we've come and appreciate what we have. It is hugely satisfying all these years later to see how the current staff embodies the foundational ethos that developed so organically in the early years of the firm. All along we have been dedicated to creating great residential architecture, running a great business, and educating and serving the communities we care about. This is the common thread that binds us and holds us steady as we proceed forward."

"I AM GLAD THAT GREG PALMER CROSSED MY PATH; otherwise, he'd be a formidable competitor. You can bet he'd be successful in anything he put his mind to. Greg doesn't need my endorsement, but I have had the distinct honor of getting to see him grow from a young upstart to an elegant architect managing this "upstart" of a company. 'If I leave here tomorrow,' I'd rest peacefully knowing Greg is looking after the shop."

—BILL HARRISON, 2016

PLATE 35

PLATE 36

PLATE 37

PLATE 38

PLATE 39

PLATE 40

PLATE 41

PLATE 42

PLATE 46

PLATE 47

PLATE 48

PLATE 49

PLATE 50

PLATES 51–54

PLATE 55

PLATE 56

PLATE 57

98   EARLY GROWTH

PLATE 58

PLATE 59

PLATE 60

PLATE 61

PLATE 62

PLATE 63

PLATE 64

Richard C. Hatch

Deepening the Bench

A Wisconsin native, Rick Hatch spent many childhood summers with his family near Spring Green, Wisconsin, which is the location of Frank Lloyd Wright's Taliesin East. A Wright-designed school, restaurant, and several small cottages were also nearby and along with Taliesin East, became Rick's earliest architectural influences, indelibly imprinting Wright's example of marrying a building to its site. In spite of his interest in architecture, however, Rick began his academic career studying forestry, thinking that he would follow in his father's footsteps.

After three years, Rick decided that forestry was not satisfying enough to become his life's work and he took a sabbatical to travel abroad and consider his path forward. Upon returning to the United States, while bartending and ruminating on what to do next, his thoughts eventually returned to architecture. Sparked by the memory of the architectural tours of his youth, which were led by the Frank Lloyd Wright Foundation, he also realized that his background in forestry had developed his propensity to read a site well. It clicked. Focus thus adjusted and restored, Rick resumed his studies, completing dual degrees in Architectural Engineering and Architecture at Southern Polytechnic State University.

When Rick arrived at Harrison Design Associates in 1998, he deftly took on the opportunities that came his way and discovered he had an aptitude for encouraging clients to articulate what they envisioned for their homes. He says, "I was a bartender for seven years while I completed my education. I love to talk to people and listen to what they have to say. I think every architect would benefit from this kind of interaction with people. While bartending, I honed a communication skill intrinsic to the practice of architecture. I also have a good repertoire of jokes, which comes in handy."

Proud to serve as a designer for several generations of families, Rick truly values the relationships he's made over the years. Kind, chivalrous, and

honorable, it is clear that the feeling is mutual among Rick's clients and colleagues alike who always feel validated and valued in his presence. Reflecting on the moments during his career at Harrison Design that made him stop short and take stock of his profession he says, "The responsibility given to us, and the certitude of our clients that we can imagine what is possible and make it happen is powerful. I love to work out solutions in the midst of conversation or walking a site, sketching all the while." Rick sees possibility in every opportunity; every potential project has merit. Like Bill Harrison, he thoughtfully sketches upside-down for clients to illuminate an idea or concept with ease.

Rick adds, "I'd say that Bill and I are sort of dreamers and can get carried away, but we know that we can be ourselves. We share very similar, somewhat circuitous professional routes, which color how we practice. Sometimes Greg Palmer or John Albanese, who are more practical, reel us in. It is a good balance and we have the kind of open relationship that makes it work."

Inspired by the work of southern-based classicists Philip Trammell Shutze and Neil Reid, and Britain's Sir Edward Lutyens, Rick is passionate about details. Every element he designs, whether a door surround, portico, dormer, soffit, or chimney reveals Rick's thoughtful consideration of proportion. For him, each component is integral and completes a statement about the architecture. Known for his intuitive space planning, Rick tunes into visual balance for effective massing as well as the use of ornament.

Rick good-naturedly (but meaningfully) can go into a diatribe about computer rendering. While he certainly accepts and utilizes the computer, Rick believes nothing can replace drawing by hand to really work out a design. "What does that chimney cap need to look like? How does each element relate to the other? These parts are frequently slapped onto so many houses—crap on crap because they haven't been properly considered through drawing. Makes me crazy as I drive around." He and Bill like to say, "In the country of the blind, the one-eyed man is king," and are both purposeful and resolute in improving the residential built environment with every Harrison Design project.

On the future of the firm he says, "We have been talking for a number of years about what the next generation looks like and the generation after that. We are in a good position with Greg Palmer, John Albanese, Tony Spann, and me as the second generation and it is up to us to groom the generation that

"WE CONTINUALLY MENTOR EACH OTHER AND OUR NEW HIRES—WE THINK A LOT ABOUT HOW THE FACE OF HARRISON DESIGN WILL EVOLVE. IT WAS BILL'S GENIUS, OR INSIGHT, OR BLIND INSTINCT AND ABILITY THAT DIRECTED THESE LAST TWENTY-FIVE YEARS. TOGETHER, WE ARE THE BEST FIRM WE CAN BE. WE ARE IN A GOOD POSITION TO GO ANOTHER TWENTY-FIVE YEARS."

follows. Bulent Baydar, Chad Goehring, and Jesse Harrison have experienced the work ethic, and those that come behind them will inherit a successful operation. It is something we are all mindful of."

"We continually mentor each other and our new hires—we think a lot about how the face of Harrison Design will evolve. It was Bill's genius, or insight, or blind instinct and ability that directed these last twenty-five years. Bill built the firm and our culture. Now, all of us who are in leadership roles have considerable room to transition and grow the various aspects of the business and we each play a significant part to maintain equilibrium and stability. Together we are the best firm we can be. We are in a good position to go another twenty-five years."

"AN OLD ENGLISH NURSERY RHYME HAS A LINE, '…and he shall have music wherever he goes…' With Rick, one might say 'he shall have laughter wherever he goes.' People simply enjoy being around him. His clients love him; his employees respect him. I'm glad his journey finally led him to do what he was born to do. His designs are beautiful and his economy is elegant."

—BILL HARRISON, 2016

PLATE 65

PLATE 66

PLATE 67

PLATE 68

PLATE 69

PLATE 70

PLATE 71

PLATE 72

PLATE 73

PLATE 74

PLATE 75

PLATE 76

PLATE 77

PLATE 78

PLATE 79

PLATES 80–83

PLATE 84

PLATE 85

John J. Albanese

Success: Nonstop From Atlanta to New York

Architect and principal John Albanese joined Harrison Design in 1999. There were eleven employees at the time, including Greg Palmer, Rick Hatch, and Bulent Baydar. At the time, ninety-five percent of their work was in Georgia, and ninety percent of that was in Atlanta. In the decade to come, those statistics would change dramatically with the firm's outpost offices in California, St. Simons Island, Washington, DC, and New York, as well as international projects that saw the firm through the economic downturn in 2008. The firm also began to have more influence over better design and building practices.

A native of Long Island, New York, John attended the University of Kentucky for his undergraduate studies and Virginia Tech for his Masters of Architecture. He began his career in New York doing residential work for a couple of small boutique offices. In 1997 John left New York to work in a residential architecture firm in Atlanta and later found his way to Harrison Design Associates.

Of those early days, John recalls, "It was a luxury to work directly with Bill. There were lots of Saturdays and late nights, but I realized I had arrived at a unique place. I felt at home and embraced the circumstances to learn directly from Bill—his philosophy and work ethic, his passion—I had a real advantage compared to my peers at other firms."

Appointed to run one of the Harrison Design studios at an early age, John continued to develop his management and design skills. In 2009, along with Rick Hatch, John became a principal at the firm and together with Greg Palmer and Bill Harrison they took on the responsibility to develop and grow the firm. Even then, as Greg Palmer noted, leadership began to look critically at the operations of the firm on a daily level as well as long-term.

After the St. Simons office opened in 2006 and the DC office was well-underway, a New York office began to take shape in 2012 under the direction of John and another Long Island native, Bernard Austin,

who had previously worked in Harrison's Santa Barbara office. Together with their combined knowledge of the New York region and the Hamptons, Bernard and John created and ran the office. When Bernard moved on, John remained committed to the development and cultivation of the office even as he continued living and working in Atlanta, where he also had projects. As a firm principal and as a New Yorker, he was personally vested in seeing the office succeed, and for well over a year managed to be two places at once. John subsequently helped negotiate a merger with a New York architect named Matthew Korn, who became the Managing Principal of the Harrison Design New York office in late 2015.

Disciplined and affable, John derives great satisfaction from working in residential architecture and loves engaging with clients to help them achieve their dreams.

"We are so hands on and work inclusively with homeowners every step of the way to create the best experience for everyone: client, architect, builder, community. Working with an architect can be pleasurable and successful. We know it is often a leap of faith for clients—everyone only hears how wildly frustrating the process can be—but it can also be one of the best milestones in their lives. We want our clients to never stop talking about their positive experience."

While every architect aspires to make a difference, John takes the adage to heart and elaborates; "To be invited into someone's life to create the place where they will 'do' their lives and raise their families is huge. We do not take this privilege lightly. It is intimate. This kind of trust is given to us and we work in concert to protect that trust. We educate along the way and advocate for our clients. We get to solve problems they may have had in previous homes and we get to give definition to their thoughts and words with our designs. By the end, it is so satisfying to see the final product, which for us isn't just a house. It is about happy people. It is elegant. It is life."

John remarks further, "We have expanded the firm's presence, not in size, but in experience and influence and we are seeing a shift. We are all on board with the emerging level of high-end residential work. Our clients are focused on doing things right, which is fantastic for us. We are able to have quality projects that are more involved and integrated. Not bigger projects, but better. The mindset has changed in general due to the Internet. It changes how clients prepare for a project. They can be more engaged in the project and are more knowledgeable; they bring binders of what they love or don't love from Houzz or Pinterest. It is a very different process now and better in general for the profession."

For John, residential work is endlessly interesting. He now mentors the firm's young interns the way Bill mentored him. "The company is only as good as its employees. Bill took the time to teach me so I take the time to pass along what I know." In addition to his practice at Harrison Design, John sits regularly on local review boards, with the goal

> "To be invited into someone's life to create the place where they will 'do' their lives and raise their families is huge. We do not take this privilege lightly. It is intimate."

of preventing poorly designed architecture from being built.

About the firm culture, John notes several aspects that make the firm special to their employees. "First," as he explains, "most schools of architecture include at least a semester to study abroad, so in general, architecture students get the bug to travel early. At Harrison Design, travel is encouraged as a personal and professional necessity. Principals and project architects frequently go on trips to learn and have first-hand experiences together." These opportunities inspire confidence, boost morale, and bonds coworkers and colleagues.

Secondly, at Harrison, people stay. Of the forty-five employees that make up seven studios at the Atlanta office alone, twenty-five individuals have been with the firm ten years or more. John continues, "We try to make it attractive for people to stay. Thanks to Deborah Harrison's foundational work, we offer terrific benefits as well. We give the responsibility, we teach, we encourage. If a young graduate has the desire and passion, he or she could become part of the firm for a long time, which in turn creates security for the firm's future."

"Thirdly, in spite of the challenges and the days that are just plain awful, there is always back up. If any of the studios get overwhelmed, whether in Atlanta or elsewhere, there is always someone to consult with on anything that might come up. It isn't a competitive environment and everyone works on issues together. The firm has an intellectual capital that is an asset for all."

The common thread is tied to Bill Harrison and his investment in the firm and his staff. As John notes, "In 2008, when the work load and opportunities dropped for everyone in the industry, we didn't have all our eggs in one basket. We had areas that were still going that kept us afloat. When I look at the chronology of our work over the years, and especially during the downturn, I am so proud to have had a part."

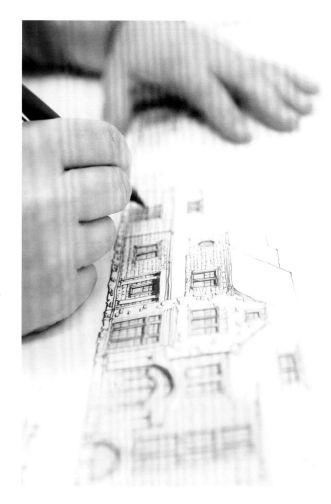

"TO THE SISTERS OF ST. LAWRENCE the Martyr Catholic School: John Albanese turned out well. I suspect your knees grew calloused and spirits grew weary during his childhood, but I wanted to say thank you. John has actually followed in your footsteps and is a gentle, encouraging teacher and coach to our newer practitioners. The words you punished him for saying, he now knows in twenty languages. But he still manages to keep the rest of us in check… and his heart is pure gold."

—BILL HARRISON, 2016

PLATE 86

PLATE 87

PLATE 88

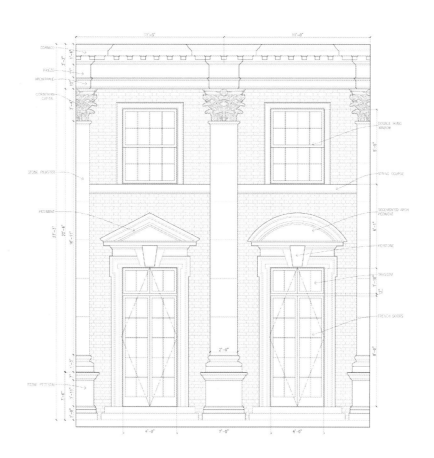

PLATE 89

PLATE 90

PLATE 91

150   EARLY GROWTH

PLATE 92

PLATE 93

PLATE 94

PLATE 95

155

PLATE 96

PLATES 97—100

157

PLATE IOI

PLATE 102

PLATE 103

PLATE 104

PLATE 105

PLATE 106

PLATE 107

PLATE 108

PLATE 109

"SHORTLY AFTER SHE GRADUATED from college, Bill hired Karen Hayes (now Ferguson) to be my assistant. As far as I was concerned, she had an Interior Design degree, which meant she knew our architectural language and would have a short learning curve. As far as she was concerned, Harrison Design Associates provided a nice platform for her to learn the trade and I believe she had her sights set on creating her own studio long before we realized what a good idea it was. We haven't regretted the first moment of having a multiple award winner in our company."

—GREG PALMER, JUNE 2016

Interiors Studio (left to right): Karen Ferguson, Director of Interior Design; Betsy McBride, and Laura Hermes.

PLATE 110

PLATE III

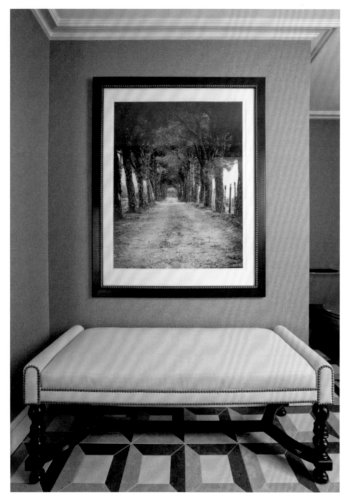

PLATE 112

PLATE 113

PLATE 114

PLATE 115

PLATE 116

PLATES 117–118

PLATE 119

PLATE 120

PLATE 121

PLATE 122

PLATE 123

PLATE 124

3

WESTWARD
EXPANSION

Anthony P. Spann

Defining the West Coast Practice

Senior Principal, Tony Spann, has managed Harrison Design's Santa Barbara location since he merged his business with HDA in 2004. In 2016, Tony continues oversight in Santa Barbara and in Los Angeles as well, where the firm opened an office in 2007.

While he was growing up, Tony's large, close-knit family lived in a Frederick Law Olmstead suburb of Chicago. His father, an engineering teacher and frustrated architect, was as much an influence on Tony's youthful aspirations as the architectural legacy of his hometown. Tony's father took him to see the old residential neighborhoods, the iconic buildings by Louis Sullivan, the University of Illinois Circle Campus, new high-rises like the John Hancock and Sears Towers, and Burnham and Root's Masonic Temple. Tony was captivated by it all.

An architecture graduate of the University of Illinois, Tony joined forces with two of his brothers, who had begun a construction business in idyllic Santa Barbara, California. In his newly adopted state, he became licensed and opened his own office, which grew over the years to a mid-sized firm with a reputation for a diverse residential and commercial practice. In the early days of practicing in Santa Barbara, studying the city's history and restoring its buildings became a hobby for Tony, and eventually, as word spread of his knowledge, people began to come to him for his expertise in historic preservation.

After twenty years in the area, the opportunities available in a relatively small geographic region proved to be harder to come by. Tony met Bill Harrison at the time of the *Traditional Home* show house and together they determined that Tony's accomplishments and connections to the area combined with his established and skilled staff, were together an ideal combination for expanding Harrison Design's reach and for giving Tony the support he needed to focus on building an expanded client base.

Tony acknowledges his father for instilling in him a few basic truths that continue to shape his work. "Dad said, 'You don't have to reinvent the wheel, but

you do have to understand history to understand how buildings—all kinds of buildings—were designed and built to be any good at designing buildings today.'"

Tony reinforces what his colleagues have observed; "It is an exciting time to be reflecting on Harrison Design's trajectory. Building on Bill's passion and fearlessness, we have become better architects and are busier than ever. Our clients have also become increasingly intelligent. The days of DIY architecture have been replaced with the realization, in general, that an architect is necessary to guide, coach, and demonstrate what it takes to design and build a house right."

Tony continues, "When clients know what to ask for, we are ready to dovetail with their enthusiasm to give them what they want. If they don't exactly know, we are experts in counseling families through the process—understandably perceived as daunting—to create a good experience, which leads to a good outcome."

Lastly he adds, "I am delighted by the awards and acknowledgment we have received over the years, especially when considering the downturns, which were so hard. It is pretty fantastic and it all comes from having great people with whom to collaborate from Bill and our compatriots in all the Harrison Design offices; my California colleagues; all our great clients, and the builders and craftspeople who together make it a joy to come to work every day."

PLATE 125

A RECENT PROJECT that holds a dear place in my heart is the historical remodel of Crocker Row No. 5 in Santa Barbara, California. Its story begins with a wonderful client who possessed clear goals and a focused mission, which was to restore the 1895 original residence and erect three accessory structures; an outdoor dining patio with trellis; a storage and mechanical building; and a two-car garage.

As there were no original drawings and the structure had been modified over the years, the client insisted upon meticulous documentation of the existing conditions focusing on the historic fabric and original components. This task alone involved our entire Santa Barbara office—a rare occurrence indeed and one that brought us all together to take care of a long neglected piece of history.

The educational component alone was a project within itself. Once the community realized the extent and goals of our work—our permits were part of the public record—people rallied behind us and offered support in many ways. This led our firm on a multi-year detour during which we worked closely with the City to develop Historical Analysis and Educational Seminars. A resulting set of Published Guidelines was incorporated into the City's current Development Standards.

The project also benefitted from a consultant contingent and a general contractor that understood and completely embraced our client's vision. This allowed the project to run very smoothly and efficiently. The end result is a magical turn back of the clock

189

as we celebrated fine turn-of-the century use of materials, craftsmanship, and attention to detail.

The historical preservation component culminated in the inaugural, and unsolicited, 2014 City of Santa Barbara Edwards & Plunkett Award for Historic Preservation, which was quite an honor for our firm. We were so proud to be nominated by the community at large and voted upon by a blind panel. It was a rare moment that surpassed the typical competitiveness usually associated with such an award.

Perhaps because this project and its achievements were recently celebrated it comes to mind so easily. Or perhaps this was simply a congruence of myriad constraints, influences, dreams and desires culminating at the right place, in the right time, and with the right people. This is certainly one of my favorite projects, one that we all try to emulate each and every day as we enjoy our practice. No doubt the next time this question is posed to me, one of our current on-the-boards projects will emerge as yet another touchstone.

—TONY SPANN, APRIL 2015

Above (left to right):
Nick Chatwatanasiri, Bill Harrison, Dan Formanek (Giffin & Crane), Tony Spann, Barbara Lowenthal, Anthony Grumbine, and Geoff Crane (Giffin & Crane).

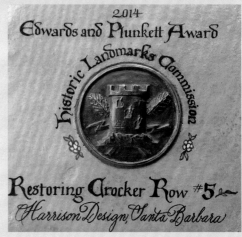

"IF YOU EVER FIND YOURSELF IN A FOXHOLE, you want Tony Spann with you. The man is a Clydesdale. Solid and dependable, his heart is roughly the size of the Midwest. Lots of people describe our company as a family. If that is case, then Tony is the beloved father figure. I am so grateful he looks after our folks out west."

—BILL HARRISON, 2016

PLATE 126

PLATE 127

PLATE 128

PLATE 129

PLATE 130

PLATE 131

PLATE 132

PLATE 133

PLATE 134

PLATE 135

PLATE 136

PLATE 137

PLATE 138

PLATE 139

PLATE 140

PLATE 141

PLATE 142

PLATE 143

212   WESTWARD EXPANSION

PLATE 144

PLATE 145

214   WESTWARD EXPANSION

PLATES 146–147

PLATE 148

PLATE 149

PLATE 150

PLATE 151

PLATE 152

Barbara C. Lowenthal

Interior Design: West Coast

arbara Lowenthal is a Senior Associate at the California offices of Harrison Design. She established and directs Harrison Design's interiors department in Santa Barbara and Los Angeles. An expert on landmarks guidelines as well as an interior designer, she has masterfully contributed to the growth and direction of the west coast offices since 2005.

Barbara's career in design emerged when she remodeled her own house. Her contractor suggested that she pursue her skill and enthusiasm for the construction and design business in some way and she did. In 1991, she established her own interior design practice, Barbara Chen Lowenthal Design, in Santa Barbara. Her interest in and concern for historic properties led to appointments on Santa Barbara's Historic Landmarks Commission and City Planning Commission. In due course, Barbara became the Planning Commission Chair, and worked with city planners and officials to develop Santa Barbara's Urban Design Guidelines. These design guidelines address the historic character, pedestrian-friendly qualities, and exemplary architecture within the urban grid of Santa Barbara.

During the 1990s, Barbara met architect Tony Spann, Harrison Design Senior Principal, while serving on the Historic Landmarks Commission for the City of Santa Barbara. They became friends and colleagues and when Tony began to work with Bill Harrison in 2004, Tony frequently called upon Barbara to consult with their clients. Greatly impressed with Barbara's skill and experience, Bill invited her to come work for Harrison Design, and the rest is history.

Of the firm's twenty-fifth anniversary Barbara observes, "Milestones like this allow us to take a moment to reflect on the breadth of the work by Harrison Design, particularly in the last ten years. The firm's previous two books primarily showcased its traditional work in the southeast, but as of 2016, the firm can present a more stylistically diverse body of work located around the country, notably in California, Washington, DC, and New York."

From Barbara's perspective as she watched other firms downsize or close during the economic decline, Harrison Design remained open and keeps going due to the firm's ability to address each opportunity to design for clients in any style, in any part of the country. The family aspect across all the offices and the ready support from the Atlanta location creates an inclusive creative culture, even for the offices in

California, which are on a different time zone, and are geographically so different. All this bodes well for the future.

Barbara observes, "In Santa Barbara and Los Angeles the clientele has steadily broadened, but the two places and our clients in both couldn't be more different. I go with it and discover something new every week. Together we strive to make the details and systems work for our clients, wherever they are, and the managing of everything runs the gamut. The vitality of the job is hugely rewarding as a result."

In addition to her successful ventures to date, Barbara was a founding member of the Pearl Chase Society, a nonprofit organization established in 1995, which is dedicated to preserving Santa Barbara's unique architecture, landscapes, and cultural heritage. She says, "I was proud to be part of such an amazing group that worked very, very hard at the city and county levels. We learned so much and successfully engaged our community to effect tangible change."

This critical experience combined with extensive presentations to the Historic Landmarks Commission broadened her appreciation and expertise of architecture, planning, and history. In 2007, Barbara was recognized by the City of Santa Barbara with its "St. Barbara Award" for her work in historical preservation.

In her twenty years in the business, Barbara notes that John Saladino has perennially been one of her great influences for successful and evocative rooms across a stylistic range. "There is so much to admire about his work. I always find something, whether a

calming sense of order or the details in a drapery, to translate into a quality appropriate for our clients."

She continues, "In LA, we are so pleased with the increase of work and such wonderful projects. It is a nice time to grow. I was glad to be a part of Santa Barbara's growth, and now I am excited to help define and shape where the firm is going in LA. It is a bigger and different marketplace and although it took longer to establish our name in LA than in Santa Barbara, we are making great progress."

"I FEEL LIKE JUST GETTING TO SAY that I know Barbara Lowenthal ratchets up my class factor by about a hundred notches. Barbara is a rare combination of intelligence, wisdom, and wit. She can advise preservationists one minute and record a DubSmash the next, without missing a beat. In eleven years I have not known her to make a misstep. I'm pretty sure she is flawless."

—BILL HARRISON, 2016

PLATE 153

PLATE 154

PLATE 155

229

PLATES 156–159

PLATE 160

PLATE 161

PLATE 162

PLATE 163

PLATE 164

PLATE 165

PLATE 166

PLATE 167

PLATE 168

PLATE 169

4

FURTHER AFIELD

Bulent A. Baydar

Canary in the Coal Mine

Bulent Baydar joined Harrison Design Associates shortly after graduating from Georgia Institute of Technology, where he earned both his bachelor and master's degrees in architecture. Twenty years later, Bulent is a principal and reflects on the opportunities that came his way, what he loves about residential design, and how he became HDA's, "canary in the coal mine" for establishing the firm's presence in California and Washington, DC.

Hired a day before Greg Palmer in August 1995, Bulent became the sixth member of the staff at Harrison Design Associates. They had a huge volume of projects compared to their small workforce and all the drawings were done by hand. It was an exciting, challenging time. As a result, long hours notwithstanding, it was an intensive continuation of Bulent's education. He acknowledged how hard and passionately Bill and Greg worked and realized he had landed in a unique place. Bumps and bruises along the learning curve were the norm, but each step, as coached by Bill and increasingly by Greg, allowed him to grow. Bulent notes, "It was exhilarating to have their confidence and mentorship. I think they saw possibilities in me that I was unaware of. It was a gift. All these years later, I am now in the position to give back to the firm by means of mentoring those who have come behind me."

Greg says of Bulent, "He had the makings of a very good architect. We needed him to rise quickly, and he didn't disappoint. When we were ready to launch the firm's presence on the west coast, Bulent was by then in an ideal place—professionally and personally—to represent us."

So in late 2003, Bulent decamped to California. The *Traditional Home* magazine show house was by then underway and he had already been flying back and forth to handle the permitting process in Montecito. When the show house opened, he served as a docent of sorts and his presence there was critical. It was a close-knit community not particularly eager for newcomers, but his mild manner and friendliness put people at ease. It helped too that the firm had al-

ready designed and overseen construction on the west coast for several Atlanta-based clients, who were very supportive. Subsequently, when Tony Spann and Bill joined forces in 2004, Bulent left the leadership of the new office in Tony's experienced hands.

In 2005, with several ongoing projects in the Washington, DC area and the *Southern Accents* show house in McLean, Virginia, Bulent again was the man on the ground. He established an office with Greg regularly joining him in the studio and in the field. Ultimately, a local architect, Mark Hughes, took over the office in 2012 and became its managing principal in 2014, where he continues to grow the firm's mid-Atlantic client base.

Bulent says, "I think as much as we all bring our own talents and personalities to the table, we have a lot in common. We each have enough ego to be confident, but not so much that we can't work cohesively. There is definitely a 'we' mentality and accountability in everything we do. We enjoy the camaraderie; there are so many talented people with whom to share ideas and information. That's the beauty of working in a large firm such as ours. We are stronger as a group."

When Bulent finished architecture school, he thought he would do urban commercial architecture, but an early colleague who worked at Harrison, convinced him to try residential work. Because the firm was so small at the time, Bulent wound up with a lot of responsibility, discovered that the personalization of residential design tapped into his creativity, and hasn't looked back.

Musing on what lies ahead for Harrison Design, Bulent emphatically states that besides the firm's reach and breadth of collective knowledge, its strength is

"WE ENJOY THE CAMARADERIE; THERE ARE SO MANY TALENTED PEOPLE WITH WHOM TO SHARE IDEAS AND INFORMATION. WE ARE STRONGER AS A GROUP."

that it is not tied to any particular style. A trend that he sees emerging shows that many clients still want a classic exterior, but desire a more open interior than a traditional floor plan might provide. Lifestyles today prompt planning for connectivity and togetherness. The exterior still informs the interior, but designs can accommodate a light-filled plan for how people want to live now as well as unify indoor and outdoor spaces. Bulent says, "Even as we are deeply rooted in traditional forms, we have the talent to give our clients what they want, regardless of the style, and can create a well-designed, well-built, wonderfully-detailed house that contributes to the built environment."

"I love forging partnerships with our clients. They are more knowledgeable than ever. Oftentimes, they arrive ready to articulate what they want, which gives the architect more direction. They inspire me to do my best and it is fun."

As the firm's work and profile has garnered national attention and awards for its intelligent thoughtful work, Bulent views the awareness as a springboard for what Harrison Design will do in the future. "We have the capacity to get the best projects around the country and have a marvelous advantage in the way we are set up. The Atlanta office is the hub, supporting the regional work there as well as the

offices around the country. The Atlanta studios provide whatever you need: renderings, back office support, a supportive office culture, and the sense of belonging to something great. The satellite offices have their own studios and a lot of autonomy, but we operate with an undivided standard."

In conclusion, Bulent hopes this commemorative book demonstrates Harrison Design's service to their clients, and the firm's ability to create beautiful homes, large and small, regardless of style. Modern designs benefit equally from the firm's collective knowledge of classical and traditional theory and elements. And most importantly, as he says, "this book is an homage to our clients, many of whom come back to us. Without them, we have no purpose."

"FOR A TURK WHO LEARNED ENGLISH by watching cartoons, Bulent Baydar's architectural literacy is spectacular. He has a natural genius for beautiful design. I am so glad that he didn't pursue commercial work. Plus, he's a Georgia Tech man. Gotta respect that."

—BILL HARRISON, 2016

PLATE 170

PLATE 171

PLATE 172

PLATE 173

PLATE 174

PLATES 175–176

PLATE 177

PLATE 178

PLATE 179

PLATE 180

PLATE 181

PLATE 182

PLATE 183

PLATE 184

PLATE 185

PLATE 186

PLATE 187

PLATE 188

PLATE 189

PLATE 190

PLATE 191

PLATE 192

PLATE 193

PLATE 194

PLATE 195

PLATE 196

PLATE 197

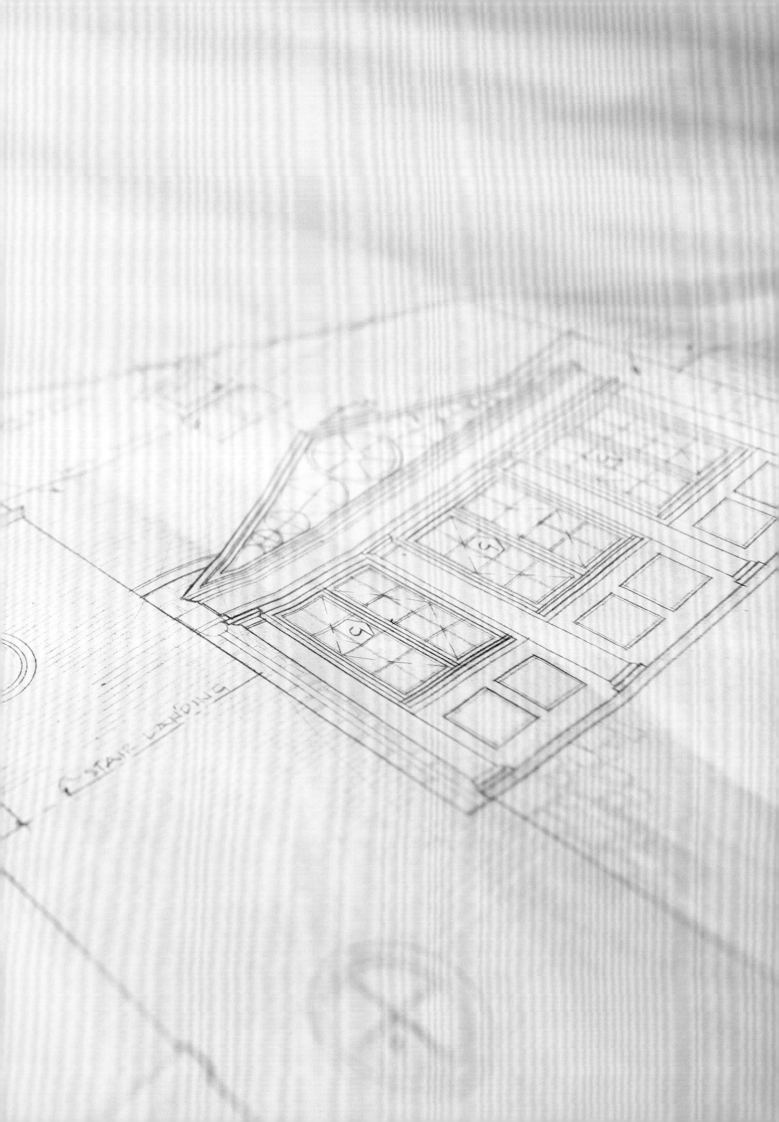

Chad E. Goehring

Establishing St. Simons

Chad Goehring is the managing principal for Harrison Design's St. Simons location, the second office to open outside of Atlanta. Handpicked for the role, Chad's disposition, professional experience, and accommodating nature is ideally suited to the island environment where he is in charge of operations, business development, client relations, assembling project teams, and construction administration. Known to hold the occasional meeting on the golf course, Chad is all business when it comes to residential architecture.

Chad began working at Harrison Design in 1998 while he was a fifth-year architecture student at Southern Polytechnic State University. After he graduated (BA, Arch) and worked six years with the firm, he was selected to take the company's operations to St. Simons Island. Several years later in 2012, he was named principal.

Chad keenly recalls being mentored during his Atlanta years, first by Bill Harrison and later by Greg Palmer. Between their efforts, Chad says that working at Harrison Design was an extension of his education and for him, full of opportunity. "I knew from the time I was a kid that I wanted to be an architect who designed houses. When you are hired at Harrison, you become part of the family and if you are eager for the responsibility, you get it. The advantage of working in a big office is that there is so much knowledge all around you." Chad availed himself to his circumstances, increasingly represented the firm at public events, brought in clients, and participated in the weekly project architect meetings.

In 2006, when Chad was 28, Greg asked him to consider moving to St. Simons to open and run an office there for Harrison Design. By then, the firm was poised to expand to serve other markets. The Santa Barbara office was thriving and the firm's loyal Atlanta-based clients created a demand for luxury vacation homes in coastal communities. It was a natural progression. Chad continues, "Without a doubt, it was a wonderful offer. Working for Harri-

son already felt exactly right. It was home to me and I got to make the St. Simons office an extension of that. My decision to take it on has been great both professionally and personally."

Increasingly, the firm's reputation comes not only from its past track record, but also from the rising talent, experience, and knowledge within the company. Chad notes, "The beauty of Harrison Design

is that we have the personnel to fill every need. The way we are set up, I can dig deeply into the design experience and have the whole firm at my back. We have incredible resources. Sure there are company politics, but thinking about being on my own with zero support is not very attractive. It is nice to belong to something. I am doing the work I always hoped to do."

Further musings: "There is so much to manage in our industry and you learn as you go. No architect goes to school thinking they'll learn about managing a business. So much of it is about having the right people on board to do what they do best. From his vast experiences, Bill is always willing to share what worked and what didn't. Everything we do is geared to make sure our clients know that we really care about them and their goals."

Chad continues, "Bill and Greg have different strengths that contribute to the make-up, tenor, and purpose of the firm. Bill is all about the big picture. He is completely unfettered and has the ability to draw elevations on the fly. He is comfortable showing the creative process to the client, which is so important for them to see. It is critical to be able to draw in front of clients to engage them in problem solving. Greg is all about the details and getting it

correct. He spends the time to capture the essence with the necessary visuals and he wows clients in his own right. He gets people to open up about their expectations, he really listens for the cues that allow us to design expressly for them."

"I have found my own path and ways to emulate them in equal measure. I think we all do. The design side for me is fun. I like talking to people about their dreams and gleaning something from how they express themselves. The relationships are so fortifying. When I get notes from our clients after they've moved in and are really living in what we created together, I am so moved to have played a part in what for many is the single most expensive investment of their lives. We say this all the time, but the responsibility and trust are huge." This is a recurring theme among the principals who have built one of the best known and respected firms, locally and nationally, from a scrappy design-build company to a sophisticated, award-winning firm.

Chad concludes, "I like to look at the past, distant and recent, to inform and create the way people live now and in the years ahead. We have a variety of work to show in this book and I think it will open eyes to what we do. We have a great time, offer great service, and are going strong. There is so much work ahead, from screened porches to whole houses—we even have a new initiative for the creation of ecclesiastical pattern books—but building relationships is the most important thing we do as architects. We get to transform lives that in turn, transform us."

"CHAD WAS REALLY YOUNG WHEN HE AGREED to move to an island and hang out the Harrison Design shingle ten years ago; I'm not entirely sure he was shaving yet. He has since then busied himself becoming a respected businessman in the Golden Isles community with a reputation for honor and integrity. I am proud of your accomplishments, Chad, but I'm more proud that you're my friend."

—BILL HARRISON, 2016

PLATE 198

PLATE 199

PLATE 200

PLATE 201

PLATE 202

PLATE 203

PLATE 204

PLATE 205

PLATE 206

PLATE 207

PLATE 208

PLATES 209—210

PLATE 211

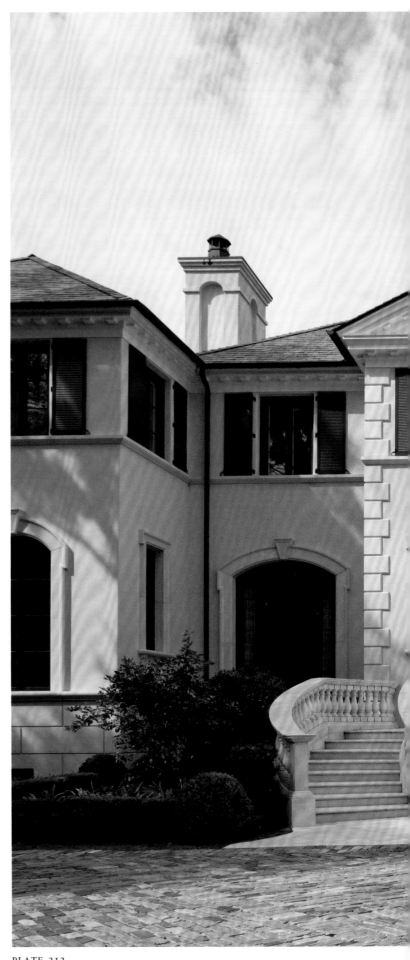

PLATE 212

PLATES 213—216

PLATE 217

PLATE 218

PLATE 219

PLATE 220

PLATE 221

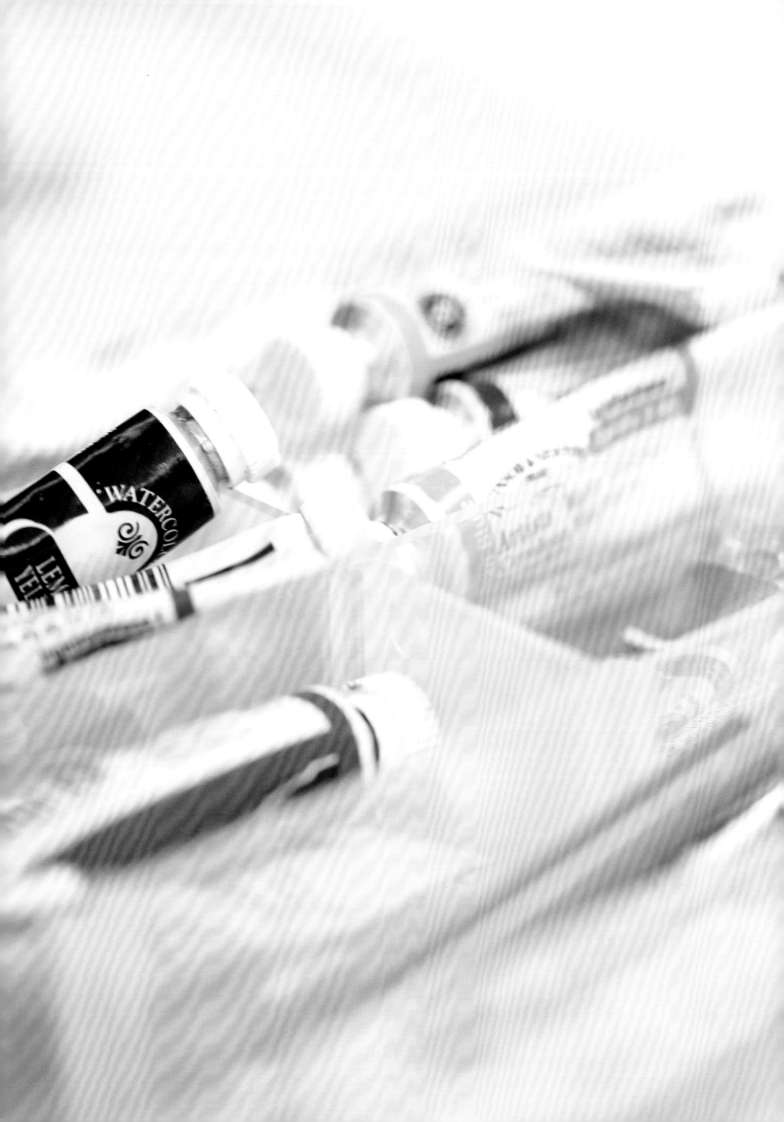

Mark D. Hughes

Mid-Atlantic Presence

A native son of Washington, DC, Mark Hughes is long-influenced by the architectural legacy and natural beauty of the mid-Atlantic region. He attended the University of Maryland where he received both his undergraduate and graduate degrees in architecture. After completing his education, Mark remained in the geographical area that first sparked his architectural interest. In 1990, Mark joined a small practice, which grew exponentially until 2009 when the recession's impact was in full force. His career prior to joining Harrison Design includes commercial, historic, retail, restaurant, space planning, and residential design.

Meanwhile, in 2005, Harrison Design was commissioned by *Southern Accents* magazine to design a show house in McLean, Virginia. The show house was hugely successful in bringing the firm name recognition and identified an ambitious new market. Greg Palmer and Bulent Baydar traveled regularly between Atlanta and Washington to establish an office while managing the growing roster of projects in Northern Virginia and the DC metropolitan area. In 2012, Harrison Design hired Mark to take over direction and operations there.

Mark notes, "I was impressed with the office and its culture. They emphasize hand drawing, which was important to me; the commissions were exciting, and the main Atlanta office with satellite configurations presented great advantages and professional opportunity. I was attracted to the autonomy and trust to run the DC office and was equally excited to gain excellent support and like-minded peers." Likewise, Mark's presence, design skill, and familiarity with the local government and jurisdictional processes has been a good fit for Harrison Design. He was named principal in 2014.

As one of the newest principals with HD, and one who has run his own practice, Mark has a deep appreciation for the firm's longevity to date. "Harrison Design has continuously found a way to create its future. The firm offers high quality services across

styles and regions without diluting its brand. I hope this anniversary book helps promote the tradition of architecture, that is to say, the tradition of continually expanding upon the classical language and design to become modern—or contemporary—to suit how we live today."

Mark's go-to sources for traditions to expand upon or adopt include the houses and gardens designed by the British architects Edward Lutyens, (as a young man, Mark worked in the Lutyens-designed British Embassy in Washington) and C. F. Voysey, who was also known for his furniture and textile designs. From Italy, the architecture of Palladio and Scamozzi are perennially inspiring. Mark also admires the work of American architects Mellor Miegs & Howe, Philip Trammell Shutze, and Frank Lloyd Wright, who he discovered while in high school. Books and monographs about all these architects are never far from Mark's desk; his shelf also includes books on shingle style and the *Architecture of the Old South* series published by the Beehive Press.

These resources and so many others are marvelous of course, but what "ups the game" for Mark at Harrison Design is that among the principals and project architects, "…there isn't a selfishness among the group. Everyone helps out and offers suggestions and manpower, and the projects benefit, not in a 'too many cooks' kind of way, on the contrary, our combined efforts come through as a unified voice."

"I am excited about the future of architecture and certainly for the firm. Energy consciousness is so relevant as are the New Green ideals and use of traditional building materials. Meshing traditional, green, and modern designs will take the firm to the next level. Our clients increasingly want their homes to be traditional, even formal, on the exterior, but reflect family-oriented comfort on the inside." Mark further projects that siting, a basic consideration long-ignored because of the advent of air-conditioning and other climate controls, is becoming more important again. "Building shelter, the idea of a house that really works, is very rewarding. It is nice to give clients more than they expect."

Motivated by this concept, Mark believes that Harrison Design, as an entity, genuinely wishes to build something good on earth for people, to the best of its collective ability. This moves him forward every day. Traveling too lifts him up. He says, "I love to see architecture by the masters. I come away with a better understanding from experiencing the work, the elements, and the surroundings. I fill up on appreciation and inspiration and draw as much as I can."

Woven throughout the personal stories in this volume are thoughts about the future for Harrison Design. Mark is proud of the DC office and its growth. He says, "I have thrived professionally. I have the freedom to do what I do well and have great collaborative colleagues. It is the greatest reward for an architect to be part of an organization that enhances the daily lives of the families and individuals that inhabit each project. I have every reason to believe that this motivation will continue to serve the firm in the years ahead."

"…THERE ISN'T A SELFISHNESS AMONG THE GROUP. EVERYONE HELPS OUT AND OFFERS SUGGESTIONS AND MANPOWER… OUR COMBINED EFFORTS COME THROUGH AS A UNIFIED VOICE."

"WHEN YOU'RE SWIMMING WITH THE SHARKS in Amity, you need a combination of Martin Brody, Captain Quint, and Matt Hooper to manage them. In what was designed to be the most intimidating city in the world, Washington, DC, you only need Mark Hughes. We are glad to have you with us, Mark."

—BILL HARRISON, 2016

PLATE 222

PLATE 223

PLATE 224

PLATE 225

PLATES 226–227

PLATE 228

PLATE 229

PLATE 230

PLATE 231

PLATE 232

PLATE 233

PLATE 234

PLATE 235

PLATE 236

PLATE 237

PLATE 238

PLATE 239

PLATE 240

PLATE 241

PLATE 242

PLATE 243

"I KNEW BILL CALDWELL professionally and had collaborated with him for years before we created a studio for Landscape Design. He and I were at lunch one day catching up and he mentioned he was looking for the next step in his career. One topic led to another and before the day was out, Bill Harrison and I offered Bill the opportunity to create a Landscape Studio for Harrison Design and he accepted. Providence has been good to us."

—GREG PALMER, JUNE 2016

Landscape Studio (left to right): William Caldwell, Landscape Studio Director; Chris Sawhill, and Sydney Thompson.

PLATE 244

PLATE 245

PLATE 246

PLATE 247

PLATE 248

PLATE 249

PLATE 250

5

GROUNDWORK
FOR THE FUTURE

Jesse J. Harrison

Expanding the National Identity

J esse Harrison is the Business Development Director at Harrison Design's Los Angeles office. Originally from Atlanta, Jesse went to school in Chicago to study design. Returning home to Atlanta, he built a career in fashion marketing then in the fine art and real estate industries. Jesse recalls driving around Atlanta's residential neighborhoods noticing a big blue sign posted at the sites where so many houses were under construction. The signs were all from Harrison Design Associates.

Even as his endeavors were thriving in Atlanta, Jesse found that he was particularly attracted to the West Coast, which felt like home to him. Over time, he began to envision what his life might look like in Southern California. He visited friends there whenever he could as he considered career possibilities. And curiously, whenever he was in Los Angeles, he noticed the same blue signs all over the place, which prompted an exciting new idea for what he might do next.

Not unlike Bill in his early years, Jesse did not hesitate to redefine his next purpose in life. He discovered that Harrison Design's LA office, then located on Wilshire Boulevard, could hardly keep up with the demand. Thus, Jesse conceived of a business development position that would take full advantage of HDA's growing reputation and the wonderful opportunities that were springing up. Jesse believed that the office would really take flight if he were on board to develop and grow the business.

Back in Atlanta after these revelations, Jesse confesses, "I was a bit of a stalker at the Harrison Design office. As I learned more and more about HDA, the more I was convinced that I was ideal for a new position in the LA office. I called Joni Diehl and Bill regularly and although it took a while, I have never forgotten when the call came from Bill for a proper interview." Jesse was in New York at the Frick Museum at that moment, which seemed to him to be a very positive sign. His persistence had paid off. When Bill asked Jesse about his strengths Jesse recalls, "I told him 'I am a master of organization, passionate about style and design, and I am good with people.' To my delight, he took a chance and hired me."

When Jesse arrived at the LA office in 2010, he called everyone he knew and the tides began to turn as he wooed and won house commissions. As a result, architect and Managing Principal, Tony Spann began to spend more time in LA along with Interior Designer, Barbara Lowenthal to execute the new work.

Within six years, Jesse was made principal and he is proud that he is the only non-architect who serves as a managing partner of the firm. He is thoughtful about his experience to date and says; "My success at Harrison Design truly originates from what has made the company a success. Bill has an amazing ability to hire people, not resumes. He trusts himself implicitly and puts his trust in his staff."

Jesse notes that Bill's enthusiasm and deep-seated entrepreneurial work ethic tends to draw people who similarly don't need a lot of supervision or constant validation. Incoming and talented people know they won't be micromanaged and that they will have a great deal of responsibility and job satisfaction. Jesse says, "It is very empowering to have Bill's confidence and I know he revels in seeing us flourish and grow to make an indelible impression—together and as individuals—on the evolution of the firm. It's a win-win situation all around."

The other special aspect of the firm that Jesse highlights is that through the intensely personal and emotional process of design and construction, their clients frequently become very close. The assurance that comes from Bill is transmitted through his principals and certainly gives their clients a sense of ease and comfort as they embark on what is for many the greatest personal investment—of time, effort and money—that they will make in their lifetime.

"It's a thrill really, to have the privilege of shaping the backdrop for how our clients want to live. I love the engagement and it is fulfilling to know that our clients enjoy us too. As a result, we have numerous repeat clients."

Looking forward to the future of Harrison Design, Jesse observes that the firm has an incredible lineup now, very much like a family with deep internal dynamics, rapport, and unconditional respect. "We care about each other and the firm and together are committed to a protocol for an eventual passing of the leadership torch. Key principals who emulate the central values that Bill espouses and who also have the skill to attract great projects give the firm solid footing ahead."

Jesse is confident that Harrison Design will continue to hire the best of the best and looks forward to competing for projects nationwide. The emerging trend is transitional in design and style, which is exciting to Jesse who notes, like Bulent Baydar and others, that many clients wish to have a traditional exterior with a more modern interior. The firm gets to be inventive and marry its collective historical knowledge with new materials and contemporary lifestyles.

"MY SUCCESS AT HARRISON DESIGN TRULY ORIGINATES FROM WHAT HAS MADE THE COMPANY A SUCCESS. BILL HAS AN AMAZING ABILITY TO HIRE PEOPLE, NOT RESUMES. HE TRUSTS HIMSELF IMPLICITLY AND PUTS HIS TRUST IN HIS STAFF."

Jesse aspires to profoundly establish the brand of Harrison Design as a national firm, which happens to be represented regionally to serve the diverse markets in each. He acknowledges that the firm's roots in the southeast and the Atlanta office offers powerful support to all the other offices, but believes that each regional office adds unique strengths to that of the whole. "We have the ability to create beautiful architecture anywhere, not just traditional homes in the south. I hope this book succeeds in demonstrating that broad appeal."

In addition to his responsibilities at Harrison Design, Jesse serves on the board and as treasurer for the Institute of Classical Architecture & Art, Southern California Chapter. Jesse is also an active member of the Los Angeles Conservancy Development Committee and is a founding member of UNICEF NextGen Los Angeles.

"JESSE IS A MASTERFUL DOT-CONNECTOR. In Malcolm Gladwell's *The Tipping Point* (Little, Brown and Company, 2006), the author uses the term 'connector' to describe people among every walk of life 'with an extraordinary knack of making friends and acquaintances.' Gladwell attributes the success of connectors to 'their ability to span many different worlds as a function of something intrinsic to their personality, some combination of curiosity, self-confidence, sociability, and energy.' That's our Jesse."

—BILL HARRISON, 2016

PLATE 251

PLATE 252

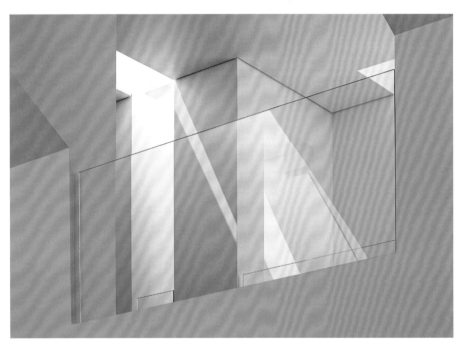

PLATE 253

PLATE 254

PLATE 255

PLATE 256

PLATE 257

PLATE 258

PLATE 259

PLATE 260

PLATE 261

PLATE 262

PLATE 263

PLATE 264

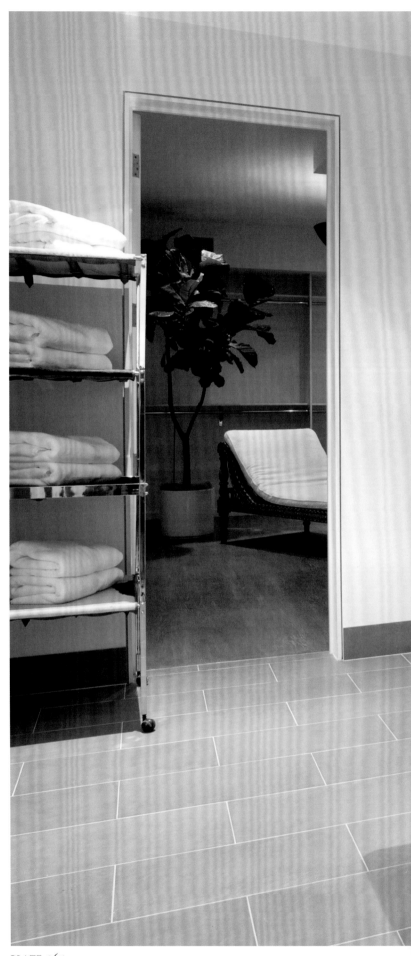

PLATE 265

PLATE 266

PLATES 267—268

PLATE 269

PLATE 270

PLATE 271

PLATE 272

PLATE 273

PLATE 274

PLATE 275

PLATE 276

PLATE 277

PLATE 278

PLATE 279

PLATE 280

6

ON THE BOARDS

VIK KROMADIT
2012

415

419

CAST CONC. WATER TABLE-
MATCH EXISTING

PORTE COCHERE
(OPEN)

A-1

A-2

A-3

BRICK VENEER T
MATCH EXISTIN

C

STONE VENEER TO
MATCH EXISTING

D

SOUTH ELEVATION
SCALE: 1/4" = 1'-0"

25

HARRISON
—— D E S I G N ——

Harrison Design at 25

1970–1989

*William H. Harrison
Establishes Client Base*

Bill founds and
creates HARRISON
CONSTRUCTION,
a successful design-build
firm serving clients in the
southeast.

1989

*Deborah Harrison takes over
Financial Leadership*

Deborah Harrison joins
Bill to provide financial
oversight and planning for
the business.

1991–1995

*Architecture Takes
Center Stage*

The architectural branch of the design-build firm grows and gains momentum as the firm's primary purpose. Bill sells the construction business and establishes HARRISON DESIGN ASSOCIATES.

1995–1998

Leadership Takes Root

Bill hires a small core of talented designers, architects, and administrators that include Greg Palmer, Rick Hatch, Bulent Baydar, and Carol Hayes.

1999

Broadening the Vision

Greg Palmer is promoted to the role of managing principal and with Bill, shares responsibility for the development and direction of the firm.

John Albanese, Derek Hopkins, Vik Kromadit, and Robbie Pich are added to the lineup of talent, thus increasing the firm's ability to project manage a growing client roster and prepare ever-more comprehensive presentation drawings and renderings.

Karen [Hayes] Ferguson establishes HDA Interior Design Division.

2000–2003

*Laying the Foundation
for Expansion*

Kazu Aiba, Chad Goehring, Robert Tretsch, Eddy Robkob, Lee [Brooks] Kinsella and Lindsay Weiss enhance the production strength of the office, preparing the way for substantial growth outside of the southeastern market.

2004

*HDA Santa Barbara
Office Opens*

Traditional Home magazine commissions HDA to design a show house in Montecito, California. The firm opens an office in Santa Barbara and Bulent Baydar temporarily moves west to open the doors. Bulent passes management of the Santa Barbara office to local architect, Tony Spann, who merges his practice with HDA.

Bryan Looney, Nicole [Haskins] Fogarty, and Josie Capps are added to the robust operation.

HDA publishes its first book, *Timeless Architecture: Homes of Distinction*, written by Elizabeth Meredith Dowling, (Schiffer Publishing Ltd., 2004).

2005

*Interior Design on the
West Coast*

Barbara Lowenthal joins HDA Santa Barbara in 2005 and establishes an Interior Design Division to serve the west coast.

Steve Markey joins HDA filling a niche for luxury commercial expertise in multi-use buildings and country clubs and adds depth to the firm's international design nexus.

2006

*HDA St. Simons
Office Opens*

The firm's Atlanta clients drive demand to the shore with commissions for luxurious vacation homes. HDA architect Chad Goehring opens and manages the St. Simons Island (GA) office to serve clients in the Golden Isles and other coastal communities in the southeast.

HDA establishes a Modern Studio at its Atlanta office. Architect Robert Tretsch leads the studio to offer concentrated response to the trend toward transitional and luxury modern design.

2007

*HDA Beverly Hills
Office Opens*

Harrison Design California opens a Beverly Hills office to more conveniently serve clients in the Los Angeles area. The office opened in 2007 and business expanded exponentially after producing the 2008 *Cottage Living* Idea Home.

Harrison Design Associates opens a commercial division to answer the call for classically designed public spaces.

HDA publishes its second book to celebrate the firms' clients and accomplishments to date.

2008

*Building a Presence
in China*

Steve Markey initiates
a relationship with
developers in China.
Steve, Greg Palmer, and
Rick Hatch establish a
practice based in Shanghai
to design single-family
homes, townhouses, and
participate in planning
strategies for new cities.

Landscape architect,
William Caldwell, joins
HDA to create the
Landscape Design Studio.

2009

*Preparing for
the Future*

John Albanese and Rick
Hatch are named HDA
principals.

2010

*HDA Washington, DC
Office Opens*

In 2005, *Southern Accents*
magazine commissioned
a show house in McLean,
Virginia, which was a
rainmaker for HDA in
that region. Bulent Baydar
relocates to open the DC
office and Greg Palmer
travels regularly for five
years to and from the
nation's capital.

2011

*HDA New York
Office Opens*

Demand in one of the few
growing markets during
the recession required a
permanent location on
the North Shore of Long
Island. John Albanese
oversees operations.

2012

Preparation for the Future Continues

Greg Palmer and Bulent Baydar hand the DC management reins to architect, Mark Hughes and Bulent moves back to Atlanta.

St. Simons' manager, Chad Goehring, is named HDA principal.

2014

A Makeover for HDA

After twenty-three years, Harrison Design Associates gets a new identity. The name is shortened to HARRISON DESIGN, a new logo and website are created, and the firm is established in Social Media.

Future leadership of the firm's ideals and vision continues to evolve: Architects Bulent Baydar and Mark Hughes are named principals.

Jesse Harrison, Business Development Director in Los Angeles since 2010, is named principal.

2015

New York Office Merger with Matthew Korn Architecture

Matthew Korn's practice and long-time associates merge with Harrison Design to more comprehensively serve the demand in New York.

2016

Harrison Design Celebrates Twenty-Five Years

The firm publishes its third book, *Harrison Design 25*, to mark the anniversary.

Acknowledgements

"Quality is never an accident; it is always the result of high intention, sincere effort, intelligent direction and skillful execution; it represents the wise choice of many alternatives, the cumulative experience of many masters of craftsmanship."

—John Ruskin (1819-1900)

A great many individuals have contributed to the success of what is known today as Harrison Design. In 2016, on the occasion of its twenty-fifth anniversary, the firm wishes to acknowledge everyone who participated and devoted their vast talents over the years. A debt of gratitude to the multitude of engineers, landscape architects, builders, millworkers, stonemasons, ironmongers, photographers, and interior designers who made their indelible mark on thousands of Harrison Design projects. The architects' designs on paper are only as good as the skill, precision, and dedication brought to bear by masters of engineering, building, and craft.

A grateful salute to every individual, past and present, who practiced or practices the art of architecture at Harrison Design. A special note of thanks to those who carry the torch of classicism in their work, whether in traditional or contemporary forms, ascribing to the Vitruvian ideal of proportion and that architecture should be solid, useful, and beautiful. Relevant today as it was in the First Century BC, these basic truths not only inform the relational proportions of design, but also support the camaraderie and goodwill among the gifted people who create the work.

Thank you one and all for making a great first quarter of a century at Harrison Design. On to the next!

Richard C. Hatch

Chad E. Goehring

Bulent A. Baydar

William H. Harrison

Matthew P. Korn

Deborah H. Harrison

Gregory L. Palmer

John J. Albanese

Mark D. Hughes

Steven L. Markey

Robert A. Tretsch

Robert C. Pich

Jesse J. Harrison

Barbara C. Lowenthal

Karen H. Ferguson

William H. Caldwell

T. Walter Greene

R. Derek Hopkins

Anthony P. Spann

HARRISON OFFICES

ATLANTA
Kazunari Aiba
John Albanese
Patricia André-Fadiran
Devin Annunzio
Bulent Baydar
Carmen Brady
Bill Caldwell
Josie Capps
Steve Cochoff
Drew Dent
Joni Diehl
Andrea Edenfield
Karen Ferguson
Nicole Fogarty
Shaun Fogarty
Walt Greene
Deborah Harrison
William Harrison
Richard Hatch
Carol Hayes
Franklin Heery
Laura Hermes
Jorge Herrera
Derek Hopkins
Annie Hutches
Mira Irlik
Lee Kinsella

Visut Kromadit
Bryan Looney
Catherine Love
Betsy McBride
Tiffany McDowell
Steve Markey
Jeremy Nash
Vanessa Nguyen
Gregory Palmer
Christopher Peterson
Robbie Pich
Paul Reynolds
Kittipat Robkob
Mariana Rocha Rodrigues
Chris Sawhill
Sarah Shields
Teresa Snider
Kristy Swann
Sydney Thompson
Robert Tretsch
Lindsay Weiss
Marc Whitley
Alan Williamson
Regina Williamson

LOS ANGELES
Vanessa Arriagada
Cerise Carleo
Jesse Harrison
Frauke Hoermann
Richard Holt
Inessa Hovhannisyan
Ryan Ibarra
Joseph Korniewicz
Austin Lomeli
Tabitha Pessanha
Tessa Platner
Elona Shishelovskaya
Anthony Spann
Bobby Strohmer
Andrew Tullis
Alina Volovik
Maksim Volovik
Gabriel Zamora

NEW YORK

Victor Enrile
Matthew Korn
John Priolo
Chris Stoddard

SANTA BARBARA

Nick Chatwatanasiri
Adele Goggia
Anthony Grumbine
Barbara Lowenthal
Serena McClintick
Patricia Strong

ST. SIMONS ISLAND

Benjamin Bailey
Sandra Dunham
Rachel Flanagan
Chad Goehring
Jessa Vogel

WASHINGTON, DC

Nic Charbonneau
Mark Hughes
Szu Molina
Hristina Stankovic

Deborah Harrison, Andrea Edenfield, Carol Hayes,
Regina Williamson, Teresa Snider, Vanessa Nguyen,
and Josie Capps
Accounting Department

William H. Harrison, Robert J. Proctor, and
Gregory L. Palmer
*Friend and mentor from the beginning, attorney Robert J. Proctor is
an honorary member of the Harrison Design family.*

Lee Brooks Kinsella, Bryan Looney, and Catherine Love
Director of Marketing, Director of IT, and Office Manager

William H. Harrison and Joni Emerson Diehl
The Founder and his Assistant

Project Credits

PLATES 65, 66, 67, 68
Photographer: Erica George Dines
Builder: McGarrity-Garcia
Interior Designer: Huff-Dewberry, LLC
Landscape: Alex Smith Garden
   Design, Ltd.

PLATES 69, 70, 71, 72
Photographer: John Umberger
Interior Designer: Meridy King Interiors
Landscape: Viridis Garden Design, Inc.

PLATE 73
Photographer: John Umberger
Landscape: Greenmark Landscaping

PLATES 74, 75, 76, 77, 78
Photographer: Fred Gerlich
Builder: Bonner Construction
Interior Designer: Jacquelynne P.
   Lanham Designs, Inc.
Landscape: Dargan Landscape
   Architects

PLATES 79, 80, 81, 82, 83, 84
Photographer: Mali Azima (79)
Photographer: John Umberger (80-84)
Interior Designer: Carla Thompson
Landscape: Ed Castro Landscape, Inc.

PLATE 85
Photographer: John Umberger
Landscape: Ed Castro Landscape, Inc.

PLATES 86, 87
Photographer: John Umberger
Builder: InTown Development
   Group, LLC

PLATES 88, 89, 90, 91, 92
Photographer: John Umberger (89, 91)
Photographer: Blayne Beacham Macauley
   (88, 90, 92)
Interior Designer: Harrison Design
Landscape: Joe A. Gayle & Associates

PLATES 93, 94, 95, 96, 97, 98, 99,
100, 101, 102, 103
Photographer: Mali Azima
Interior Designer: Joel Kelly Design
Landscape: Joe A. Gayle & Associates

PLATES 104, 105, 106, 107, 108
Photographer: John Umberger
Builder: Jim Roberts
Interior Designer: Dilger Gibson
Landscape: Land Plus Associates

Interiors Studio

PLATES 109, 111
Photographer: Christina Wedge
Builder: RHS Ventures, LLC

PLATES 110, 117, 118
Photographer: John Umberger (110)
Photographer: Joel Silverman (117-118)
Builder: AFG Builders

PLATES 112, 113
Photographer: Christina Wedge
Builder: Bildon Construction

PLATES 114, 115
Photographer: Christina Wedge

PLATE 116
Photographer: Richard Leo Johnson
Builder: MCD Construction

PLATES 119, 120
Photographer: Sarah Dorio
Builder: Sheehan Built Homes

PLATES 121, 122
Photographer: Sarah Dorio
Builder: Smith & Kennedy

PLATE 123
Photographer: Christina Wedge

WESTWARD EXPANSION

PLATES 124, 126, 127, 128, 129, 130,
131, 132, 133
Photographer: Jim Bartsch
Builder: Giffin & Crane
Interior Designer: Barry Dixon
Landscape: Katie O'Reilly Rogers

447

PLATE 125
Photographer: Jim Bartsch
Builder: Giffin & Crane
Landscape: Kris Kimpel Landscape
 Architecture

PLATES 134, 135, 136, 137, 138, 139
Photographer: Jim Bartsch
Builder: Tyler Development
 Corporation
Interior Designer: Harmony Hall
 Interiors
Landscape: Clark and White Landscape

PLATES 140, 141, 142, 143, 144, 145
Photographer: Harrison Design (140)
Photographer: Jim Bartsch (141-145)
Builder: R. J. Spann
Interior Designer: Jackie Terrell Design
Landscape: Lisa Mosely Garden Design

PLATES 146, 147, 148, 149, 150, 151, 152
Photographer: Greg Frost
Builder: Euroconcepts
Interior Designer: Harmony Hall
 Interiors

PLATES 153, 154, 155, 156, 157, 158,
159, 160, 161
Photographer: Jake Cryan
Builder: Allen Construction
Interior Designer: Harrison Design
Landscape: Grace Design

PLATES 162, 163, 164, 165, 166, 167
Photographer: Jim Bartsch
Builder: Giffin & Crane
Interior Designer: Harrison Design
Landscape: Grace Design

PLATE 168
Photographer: Paula Watts
Builder: Blackrock Construction
Interior Designer: Harrison Design
Landscape: Sydney Baumgartner
 Landscape

FURTHER AFIELD

PLATE 169
Photographer: Courtesy of West Side
 Estate Agency
Builder: Tyler Development Corporation
Interior Designer: Harmony Hall Interiors
Landscape: Clark and White Landscape

PLATES 170, 171, 172, 173
Photographer: John Umberger
Builder: Raines Brothers
Interior Designer: Susan Young

PLATES 174, 175, 176, 177, 178
Photographer: David Christensen
Landscape: Terranova Landscape Design

PLATES 179, 180, 181, 182, 183, 184, 185
Photographer: Peter Vitale (for *Veranda*)
Builder: RoseKastle, Inc.
Interior Designer: Dan Carithers
Landscape: Tunnell & Tunnell
 Landscape Architecture

PLATES 186, 187, 188, 189, 190
Photographer: Gil Stose (186-189)
Photographer: John Umberger (190)
Builder: Woodall Construction
Interior Designer: Harrison Design
Landscape: Joe A. Gayle & Associates

PLATES 191, 192, 193, 194, 195,
196, 197
Photographer: Thibault Jeanson
 (191, 192, 197)
Photographer: Philip Ennis courtesy
 of Wright Brothers Builders
 (193, 194, 195, 196)
Builder: Wright Brothers Builders
Interior Designer: Suzanne Kasler Interiors
Landscape: Joe A. Gayle & Associates

PLATES 198, 199, 200, 201
Photographer: Richard Leo Johnson
Builder: Golden Isles Custom Homes
Landscape: GreenTec Landscape

PLATES 202, 203, 204, 205, 206
Photographer: John Umberger
Builder: Jones & Jones Premier
 Builders, Inc.
Interior Designer: Harrison Design
Landscape: Joe A. Gayle & Associates

"The master in the art of living makes little distinction between his work and his play, his labor and his leisure, his mind and his body, his information and his recreation, his love and his religion. He hardly knows which is which. He simply pursues his vision of excellence at whatever he does, leaving others to decide whether he is working or playing. To him he's always doing both."

—JAMES A. MICHENER